Volume I
AN ENDURING FLAME:
Studies on Latino Popular Religiosity
Editors: Anthony M. Stevens-Arroyo
& Ana María Díaz-Stevens

Volume II
OLD MASKS, NEW FACES:
Religion and Latino Identities
Editors: Anthony M. Stevens-Arroyo
& Gilbert R. Cadena

Volume III
ENIGMATIC POWERS:
Syncretism with African
and Indigenous Peoples' Religions
Among Latinos
Editors: Anthony M. Stevens-Arroyo
& Andres I. Pérez y Mena

Volume IV
DISCOVERING LATINO RELIGION
A Comprehensive Social Science Bibliography
Editor: Anthony M. Stevens-Arroyo
with Segundo Pantoja
Foreword: Robert Wuthnow

S

Discovering Latino Religion:

A Comprehensive Social Science Bibliography

Edited by
Anthony M. Stevens-Arroyo
with
Segundo Pantoja

Program for the Analysis
of Religion Among Latinos
PARAL Series
Volume Four

Published in the United States by the Bildner Center for Western Hemisphere Studies, 33 West 42 St., New York, NY.
This publication is made possible by grants from The Lilly Endowment and The Pew Charitable Trusts.

All rights reserved under International and Pan-American Copyright Conventions. Published in the United States by the Bildner Center for Western Hemisphere Studies, 33 West 42 St., New York, NY.

Library of Congress Catalog-in-Publication Data

Discovering Latino Religion: a comprehensive social science
    bibliography / edited by Anthony M. Stevens-Arroyo.
            p. 142 cm.—(PARAL studies series:v. 4)
    Includes bibliographical references.
    ISBN 0-929972-13-9 (hbk.)—ISBN 0-929972-14-7 (pbk.)
    1. Hispanic Americans—Religion—Bibliography. 2. United
States—Religion—Bibliography
    I. Stevens-Arroyo, Antonio M., 1941-. II. Series. III. Series: Bildner
Center series on religion: v. 4.
    27757.U5D57 1995
    BR563.H57   016.2'0089'68073—dc20   95-11518
                                                                  CIP

Cover, book design and layout by André Boucher
Manufactured in the United States of America
First edition

CONTENTS

Preface

The Bildner Center for Western Hemisphere Studies sponsors research, forums, seminars and publications that address the practical resolution of public policy problems facing the nations of the hemisphere. It is part of The Graduate School and University Center of The City University of New York (CUNY). The Center serves as a link between CUNY's intellectual community and other experts and policymakers working on contemporary issues in Latin America, North America and the Caribbean, and provides a window on New York for scholars and public officials throughout the Americas. The Center was established in 1982 by the President of CUNY's Graduate School and University Center, the University's Board of Trustees, and Albert Bildner, a philanthropist with extensive experience in hemispheric affairs.

The Program for the Analysis of Religion Among Latinos (PARAL) coordinates a national effort at systematic study of religion in the experience of people of Latin American descent living within the 50 states and Puerto Rico. With its office located at the Bildner Center for Western Hemisphere Studies in New York City, PARAL promotes regional and comparative research among academics, provides information to churches and co-sponsors an annual competition for the Olga Scarpetta Award to the best student paper on Latino religion.

The PARAL series on Latino Religion is published by Bildner Center Books in New York, under the general editorship of Anthony M. Stevens-Arroyo. With grants from the Inter-University Project for Latino Research, the Lilly Endowment and the Pew Charitable Trusts, PARAL invited the leading scholars of Latino religion into a process that included a three-day conference at Princeton University in April of 1993. The four volumes of the series are the result of continued dialogue and research on key topics of scholarly inquiry.

Bildner Center Publications
Publisher: Ronald G. Hellman
Managing Editor: Peter Robertson

Foreword
Syncretism, Popular Religion, and Cultural Identity

Robert Wuthnow

The publication of four volumes by the Program for the Analysis of Religion Among Latinos is an important step in the development of the study of religion in America. This importance is not limited to the welcome addition of Latino voices in the scholarly study of their own reality or to the general need for the classroom and research library to have texts such as the first three books and this volume's social science bibliography. Clearly, the issues raised by the PARAL series provide food for scholarly thought, even among those of us who do not focus upon Latinos in our own work. In this foreword, I would like to suggest a few ways that we can all benefit from an exploration of syncretism, popular religiosity and cultural identity—the three themes of PARAL research.

Syncretism has a dual meaning in the present context. It means, on the one hand, the blending of elements from different religious traditions. Thus, the blending of ritual practices from Roman Catholicism and from Aztec religion would be an example. This, of course, comes very close to the way in which syncretism has traditionally been understood. On the other hand, it may also mean "accommodation," that is, a blending of religious and nonreligious elements. It is clear that syncretism is an issue worthy of special consideration in the Latino context—and perhaps one that should be considered more seriously in other contexts as well. But we need to be clear about why it is important.

Let me give an example. A year ago on Easter Sunday I was in Arizona. Inspired by the warm weather, I rose early and went jogging (a religious rite for many nowadays). I then turned on religious television (perhaps an example of syncretism itself). The Easter service was coming from a large cathedral in the mission style of the southwest. The triptych behind the altar was clearly a combination of Spanish Catholic and Native American design. The congregation appeared to consist of Latinos and Anglos in about equal numbers.

The presiding priest was African American. Much of the liturgy was recognizably Anglican, more so than Catholic. But midway through the homily, the priest broke into song, finishing in a style reminiscent of a black Baptist service. As the service ended, I could hear loud, amplified gospel music. But this was live. Across the rilliato from where I was staying, a small Latino Pentecostal church had set up shop in its parking lot. I wandered over and listened as the preacher picked out choruses on his electronic keyboard. One of the houses I passed on the way over had colored lights blinking on and off in the front window. There was also a prayer stick made of brightly colored yarn. Another had plastic eggs tied to the branches of a mesquite tree in the front yard. It also had a small wooden cross in the yard decorated with colored ribbons.

Syncretism? I would say so. It would seem only natural to identify the roots of these various rites and symbols, pointing out how they combine Eurocatholic practices with Mexican and Native American customs. But let me mention two other examples quickly. I was reminded of my Arizona example just a few days ago—this Easter in fact—as I passed the local Methodist church and saw a small cross on the front lawn made of branches and decorated with colored ribbons, flowers, and small toys. Hispanic influence, I said to myself. But then I looked again and thought, no, probably just a project of the children's Sunday school classes. My other example is from a recent conversation with the pastor of a large Methodist church in Indiana. Regaling me with the menu of programs at this church ("something for everybody") he mentioned that he frequently wears a yarmulke and prayer shawl when he reads the Old Testament, and does so from a scroll. Syncretism, I said to myself. But then, somehow, the word didn't seem quite right.

The point of these examples is two-fold: theoretical and methodological. The theoretical point is that syncretism is always a matter of power. The reason we find it attractive to talk about syncretism in the Latino case is that eclectic rites and symbols represent a challenge to Eurocatholicism. In my other two—Protestant— examples, this dimension is less relevant, and therefore, syncretism seems less appropriate. Yet, I would argue, syncretism makes a political statement even in these instances. It is no accident that the pastor of a large church in Indiana who wants to show how diverse his church is makes a point of telling people about the Jewish elements of his service. So, the theoretical reason for being interested in syncretism is not simply that different religious elements are being combined, or even that this combination represents some new theological perspective. It is that elements are being combined for strategic reasons—for symbolic reasons, that is, to make a statement.

The methodological point is simple. If eclecticism is everywhere, then it certainly deserves to be studied. But it must also be studied with an eye toward understanding its variety and uses. It does little good to point out that syncretism is the norm—unless, of course, one is simply trying to make a political statement about it. It does more good to understand what elements are being combined, and why. It makes special sense to understand syncretism (closest to its original meaning, I think) that involves the deliberate blending of elements from two different religious or religio-ethnic traditions. For those are most likely to involve questions of power. Thus, in my examples, it is more interesting to think about the blend of music, art, and liturgies from different religious traditions, than it is to talk about the addition of an electronic keyboard.

Moving then to popular religion. The term itself always bothers me. I suppose the opposite is unpopular religion. Yet that is probably not what we mean. I suspect we mean something other than priestly or clerical religion. So, again, there may be a political factor in the very act of emphasizing popular religion, just as there is with syncretism. Let's be honest about it. There may even be an anticlerical bias, especially when the Latino population is so poorly represented in the church hierarchy, and when many who study religion are themselves frustrated or former members of the clergy. But I want to suggest two aspects of popular religion that may seem counter-intuitive, given this anticlerical orientation. One is that the religious hierarchy may be more deeply implicated in popular religion than we like to think. Some years ago, Richard Fenn of the faculty of Princeton Theological Seminary published a small book on secularization. And he argues in that book that the clergy are often the main agents of secularization. Well, at the time, that was a revolutionary idea to me. I'd always thought the clergy were trying to stop secularization. But Fenn argued, quite rightly I think, that clergy are in the business of making short-term compromises. They say, well, that might work, or no harm in trying that. And, little by little, they sell their institutions down the slippery slope to destruction.

In the case of popular religion, the same may be true. One view is that clergy are always fighting popular religion, trying to make it conform to ecclesiastical authority. But another view is that clergy are secretly rejoicing whenever popular religion rears its ugly head. Well, they may say, at least those Pentecostal services are giving people something to think about. Someday they'll come back to the church. Or, what's wrong with people getting together in homes to pray and talk about the Bible? That's better than going out to wild parties.

So, I think there may be a dynamic relationship there worth looking at. Certainly in the Anglo population, clergy are very much behind the scenes in promoting popular religion. The pastor in Indiana, for example, brags that people in his church pretty much do what they want and take care of themselves. He's glad. That frees his time to raise money and plan bigger buildings.

The other point, however, is related. It is that popular religion is not necessarily the true source of vitality for the future of the church. If syncretism is a blending of elements from different religions, popular religion is a blending of the sacred and the secular. In an otherwise secular society, religion is likely to be popular because it accommodates to that reality. It may be rather innocent, such as using television to broadcast services, or electronic keyboards to create music. It may help in spreading the good news, reaching more people, tickling them where they itch. But the true winners may be norms of technique, pragmatism, numeric success, and what feels good.

I see much evidence of this in my research on small support groups in American religion. Many of these are Bible studies, most include prayer, and a majority are sponsored by churches and synagogues. The hope is that popular religion of this kind will be the wave of the future. People will find a deeper faith and come flocking back to the churches. This may happen. And yet, what occurs in many of these groups is more like the blind leading the blind. A serious study of stewardship turns into a bull session about the high cost of living. Prayer time focuses on "be with Uncle Harry's gallbladder." And God's existence depends on whether or not he helped you find a parking space yesterday.

Popular religion, therefore, must be subjected to empirical scrutiny. Just because it is popular, does not mean it is good. An anticlerical bias should not elevate its value, just because it is assumed to lack clerical control. Its limitations, as well as its strengths, must be considered.

And then, cultural identity. Very important. Extremely important. And so complex. If I may, I'd like to draw briefly from my book *Christianity in the 21st Century* in which I discuss identity at some length. My question there is whether the term "Christian" is likely to be an identity that people will find meaningful in the next century, and if so, why that might be. I argue that when we think of identity, usually we think of something that comes from, and belongs to, the individual. "I am a Christian," we say, or "I am a teacher." It is something we have chosen, or perhaps earned. But that way of thinking, in my view, is all wrong. Identity is conferred. It doesn't depend on individuals at all. It depends on institutions. So, in the case of Christianity, being Christian in the next century doesn't depend on a whole bunch of individuals going around deciding to be Christians. It depends on institutions that have the authority to confer that identity on individuals.

Now, in the case of the church—which, of course, is the main institution capable of conferring the identity of Christian—that authority has weakened greatly over the centuries. At one time, it could confer the identity to everyone who happened to live in a given territory. At one time, it could burn people at the stake who didn't like their identity. We have moved beyond this kind of public identification of religion and society. But despite the modernity of our pluralistic world at the end of the twentieth century, the case can be made that church authority over religious identity remains pretty strong. Churches still baptize infants, confirm teenagers, and marry young adults. They pretty much define what it means to be Christian.

The comparable point, then, for thinking about Latino religion is that identity isn't so much about individuals but about institutions. It may or may not be the church that will do this in the future. It will, however, be institutions of one kind or another—perhaps community organizations, perhaps government affirmative action programs, perhaps scholars. So, again, power is involved.

The other point about identity, though, is that it is constantly in flux. When I lived in Colorado in the 1960s, there was a strong Mexican American community. But being Mexican American meant something different than, say, being Chicano in California when I lived there a few years later, or than, say, being of Puerto Rican or Cuban ancestry does in New Jersey in the 1990s. If identity is institutionally constructed, then we need to understand the process by which these constructions come into being and how they change.

Here, I would like to make an appeal for comparative studies. Comparisons need to be made within the Latino community to see how different regions and different national origins and different generational factors operate. Comparisons also need to be made with other groups: Japanese-Americans, Muslim immigrants, or, for that matter, Mennonites or Swedish Baptists. Rabbis with whom I have met ask the same questions as Latino scholars.

Religiously, we are all pilgrims. What is our distinctive identity? How can we preserve it? What will it be in the future? Not too many days ago, my wife and I had the privilege of being in some friends' home, and as we listened to them tell about their journeys from Puerto Rico to New York to New Jersey, we felt we had much in common. Our journeys out of German and Scottish-American enclaves were not so terribly different. At the individual level, we need to understand better the pain—and the glory—of those journeys.

But (my last point) we also need to understand the meaning of cultural identity for the larger society. In the aftermath of the Cold War, it may mean less to us to be "Americans." It may become more important to be Latinos, or Irish Americans, or Jewish Americans. But, what promise will this hold? And what peril?

The promise is that people again find community. I discover what it means to be a Scottish Presbyterian or a German Baptist. You find what it means to be Cuban American or Mexican American. We learn from each other. We are freer to be ourselves. The peril is that we fly apart in all directions. The movie "Falling Down," which the Latino community in Los Angeles rightly found objectionable, may be a straw in the wind. Los Angeles becomes a fragmented, Third World city. Law and order diminishes. Blacks fight Koreans, and Anglos fight Latinos. Clearly, that is not the future we want.

So, in the midst of championing our ethnic differences, we must also be concerned about common ground. We must decide, not only to disagree, but to find principles about which we can agree. The volumes in the PARAL series make a contribution, not only to academic pursuits, but also to the larger questions of our world. Each of us as scholar must try to cast a bit more light upon how religion can be a source of the principles upon which we can construct a common future. And we, as students of religion, can foster their understanding. Love. Caring. Community. Peace. Justice. Forgiveness. We have only begun to probe the depths of these timeless—and universal—religious truths.

INTRODUCTION
Discovering Latino Religion

Anthony M. Stevens-Arroyo

Who is a Latino? Like the competing term "Hispanic" or older designations like "Spanish American" and "Spanish-speaking," "Latino" refers to persons of Latin American heritage who were either born or currently reside in the United States. Depending on how official statistics from government agencies are interpreted, there are between 22 and 26 million Latinos in the United States, a number larger than the entire population of nearly 65% of the countries of Latin America. The United States Bureau of the Census estimates that in the year 2013 there will be more Latinos than African Americans in the United States, making us the largest "minority" in the nation. Latinos are already more numerous than African Americans in several key regions of the country, so that the future is already here. New York City, Los Angeles and Miami are the model for a demographic trend that will reach its climax nationally within thirty years.[1]

Demographic considerations, however, do not constitute the major focus of this essay.[2] Examining how religion shapes the attitudes and behavior of this growing population is the task at hand. For some, religion may seem an unnecessary diversion from analysis of the culture and politics of the Latino peoples, just as others may consider Latino religion an interesting but marginal topic of general study of American religion. But because church policy often serves as a bellwether of general trends within the United States polity it is worth emphasizing that the study of Latino religion is not disconnected from a concern for the political and secular. Although the churches are voluntary institutions, they exercise a public role by influencing civic culture. A crucial question is whether the churches, which are institutions in "mainstream America," will advocate attitudes and policies that address the felt needs of Latino members. The answer to this question will affect both Latinos and the larger society of the United States in which we reside.

Latino religion is a complex reality that belies easy dismissal as a pursuit of only the very young, very old and very pious. Believers are a majority of the Latino population and church members are distributed among every regional, class, racial and ethnic grouping. Religion calls upon church members to live by moral standards, strengthen family ties, and intensify their social awareness. Conservative political positions are found in Latino religion, of course, but so too are liberal ones. In fact, somewhat like political activists who advocate government programs beneficial to Latinos or the Latin American exponents of Liberation Theology, Latino religion has its militants campaigning within the institutions to enlist more church resources for the betterment of the Latino community.[3] Today, while many secular and activist Latino organizations struggle for wider public support, the churches are perhaps the most trusted institutions among Latinos and among the few national ones to enjoy mass Latino membership. It is difficult to imagine a successful mobilization of Latinos for any social cause without the active collaboration of churchgoers. Latino religion clearly deserves considerable attention from scholars of the Latino reality not only for what it is but also for what it may become. Likewise, students of contemporary American religion cannot accurately diagnose the future of religion in the United States without assessment of the Latino presence.

Most Latinos are Catholics. Not only do Latinos outnumber Irish Americans in the church today, in some U. S. dioceses, Latinos are an absolute majority of all Catholics. But more interesting than the demographic increase of Latino Catholics has been the creation of a new kind of Latino Catholicism. Since 1967, the Catholic church in the United States has witnessed the historic development of pastoral institutions that have effectively restructured U.S. Catholicism. With a striking parallel to the 18th century Great Awakening in the English American colonies, after 1967 Latinos experienced a religious resurgence tied to social and political events. It was a movement that crystallized a new Latino religious consciousness and cultural identity.

This movement or resurgence of the 1960s and 1970s rode through the turbulent tides of social, ecclesial, cultural and political changes, arriving at a safe haven with the institutionalization of Latino religious organizations. Many of these grass-roots organizations became official agencies of Catholicism, thus insuring greater representation for Latinos. Although often undervalued in the study of U.S. Catholicism, the Latino resurgence made an effective contribution to the restructuring of the entire U.S. Catholic church. Today, alongside the English-speaking Euro-American Catholic church is a parallel Latino Catholicism with its own pastoral plan, liturgical books, planning commissions, training centers and network of theological, ministerial and lay associations. Rather than an afterthought, or mere imitation in Spanish of Euro-American institutions, these Latino organizations are uniquely expressive of the Latino Catholic reality. Without becoming secretly schismatic, theologically dissident or politically radicalized, Latino Catholicism has brought vitality, membership, cultural relevance and a clearer social justice mission to U.S. Catholicism. It is unlikely that the institutional church will jettison these successes since a rejection of Latino Catholicism would put at risk its relevance to Latino communities.

The proportions of Latinos in U.S. Protestantism are not as high as in Catholicism but they are growing, particularly in urban congregations. Within Pentecostalism, Latino congregations are rapidly multiplying with historic significance. More to the point, within Protestantism and Pentecostalism the indigenous, that is, Latino leadership, has demonstrated an ability to create parallel structures for a Latino church that is every bit as impressive as the Catholic experience. Moreover, Latino Protestant and Pentecostal leaders hold posts of relatively higher rank in their churches than the two dozen or so Latino/Hispanic bishops in Catholicism.[4] Perhaps most importantly, after centuries of bitter antagonism and rivalry, Latino Catholic and Protestant leaders in the United States are beginning to develop new kinds of cooperation wherein cultural and nationality similarities seem to matter more than denominational differences.

Latino religion is, therefore, a window on U. S. society. By examination of processes within the churches we gain insight into wider social trends. Ours is not a repetition of the historic assimilation of the Euro-American immigrant groups during the previous two hundred years. Nor are Latinos merely a brown version of the black American experience. Not fully an immigrant group, not exclusively a race, but also the product of territorial expansion and American imperialism, Latinos deserve to be analyzed as themselves and not as derivatives of other experiences. But it is easier to say what Latinos are not than to carefully analyze in a scientific way the particularities that emerge when considering our religious experiences. It has been the effort of the Program for the Analysis of Religion Among Latinos (PARAL) to provide some answers to these vexing questions. This essay is meant to provide a general summary of the three volumes of the PARAL series and introduce this fourth volume with its social science bibliography.

One of the most difficult tasks in any analysis of the Latino reality is to connect the very different currents of interdisciplinary Departments of Latino Studies on the one hand and a disciplinary bound study of American religion on the other. For instance, virtually every standard sociological text views Latinos as another immigrant group to be assimilated into the American Dream. Latino Studies, on the other hand, emphasize that our "entry" to the United States came by way of a war of conquest rather than by a long, emotional journey to a "new land" like most European immigrants. That is one reason that Latinos born as U.S. citizens often prefer not to be called Latin Americans, because that would imply birth in a foreign land with an alien citizenship or a less than legal residence in the United States. Should scholars of Latino religion side with the interpretations of the traditional social science disciplines or with those of contemporary Latino Studies? The decision is not an easy one because each perspective points to a different direction for interpreting Latino religion.

Whether to view Latinos as immigrants or as conquered peoples is often perceived as an ideological issue rather than a scholarly one. In a sense, the term "Latino" has as much a political content as a cultural one because it refers to an identity acquired within the United States.[5] But ideology aside, discovering Latino religion calls for sober review of the historical record. Undeniably, Texas and the Southwest, California and much of Colorado and most especially Puerto Rico were annexed to the United States after wars of expansion. Few like to call this phase of U.S. history imperialism, and textbooks are filled with euphemisms for the conquests of Texas, the Southwest, California and Puerto Rico, but scholars of Chicano and Puerto Rican history have made imperialism an inescapable premise. Since millions of Latinos can trace their family roots in their part of the United States to a time before it was the United States, it can be said that we were "American" before many Euro-Americans. In this sense, the first Latinos did not come to the

United States: it came to us generations ago when the stars and stripes were hoisted by conquering troops over the lands of our ancestors. Latinos found themselves subject to the laws of the U. S. because they were victims of military conquest, not on account of a personal decision to migrate across the seas. Scholars of Latino religion often share more with their colleagues in departments of Latino Studies than with faculty in traditional disciplines, and to better understand their research, it is necessary to recognize that the definition of "conquered peoples" is embedded in much of the new literature that this four volume series represents.

The issue flows into the study of religion because, as a general policy, the U.S. churches both Protestant and Catholic, identified evangelization of Texas, California, New Mexico and Puerto Rico with the elimination of vestiges of Mexican or Puerto Rican culture in the practice of religion. For Protestant and Catholic bishop alike, centuries old institutions like the Penitente brotherhood in New Mexico or practices like baptism by a mid-wife in Puerto Rico were to be strictly controlled when not actually eliminated. There were exceptions to this pattern of inferiorization of local religion by clerical officialdom, of course, but they scarcely deflect the judgment that U.S. churches contributed to the replacement of existing organizations that nourished Mexican or Puerto Rican identity with Americanizing institutions. It was a "Pious Colonialism" meant to stigmatize and suppress religious practices that had emerged over more than three-hundred years of Christianity dating back to the first encounter of native religions with Spanish Catholicism.[6] Without considering here the moral implications of such linkage of the faith to an imperialist enterprise, it needs to be stated that because this Pious Colonialism treated Latinos as conquered peoples, Latino religion has a birthright different from the Catholicism of Euro-American immigrants.

This is not to deny that today there are many immigrants to the United States from Latin America, especially Mexico. But the 1990 U. S. census showed that the majority of the people of Latin American ancestry in the United States were born here. Moreover, these immigrants become Latinos. One of the important results from the Latino resurgence was the creation of a Latino consciousness within religion during the past two decades. Newly arrived Latin Americans— true "immigrants"—have a tendency to assimilate to Latino parishes and congregations and not to the English-speaking so-called "mainstream" of U.S. churches. In so doing, the colonialist role of institutionalized religion has been largely negated. It is difficult not to come to the conclusion that the Pious Colonialism of nearly 125 years has been eroded. We still do not know the extent to which this phenomenon in religion applies to a general pattern for Latino identity, but the accumulated evidence suggests that Latinos are resisting cultural and linguistic assimilation in ways that most European immigrants seldom did.

Of course, not every affirmation of Latino identity is an unarticulated call to vindication. But the clear encouragement by many churches to preserve Latino culture and cultivate the Spanish language has political implications. This may be troubling to some and encouraging to others; but it ought to be significant to everyone. Precisely because we do not yet understand the consequences of resurrecting Latino identities through religion, we need further study. On the doorstep of the 21st century, the linkages between certain politico-cultural issues and church policy merit scrutiny. Will churches rally to defend the rights of Latino and Latin American peoples against the anti-immigrant bias in U.S. politics in the 1990s? Will the creation of a global economy wherein economic barriers between the United States and Mexico have been eliminated increase or diminish the advocacy by churches for international economic justice and human rights? Will Puerto Rico become a state of the union or move, like Quebec in Canada, towards separatism, appealing to religion as part of a Puerto Rican national identity? Will heightened Latino religious awareness increase or decrease the social and cultural distance between the Euro-American and Latino populations in the United States?

Study of Latino religion will not necessarily provide the answer to such questions, but it may offer some indicators of larger trends. That is why Latino religion needs to be discovered. In 1988, when PARAL began, eight of us hoped to establish the study of Latino religion as a new area of scholarly inquiry. It was our "field of dreams" to build a coordinated research and publication program for analyzing Latino religion. We felt that "if we built it, they would come." We anticipated that sociologists and anthropologists would recognize Latino religion as a major area for research about the relationship of a conquered people to the fabric of U.S. society. We hoped that scholars of the Latino reality in Chicano and Puerto Rican Studies would emerge from a stultifying reductionism and include religious factors in their research.

In all of this we drew strength from the high level of religious awareness among our people. Study of religion was not a cozy way of nurturing our academic careers, but the touchstone of understanding of the aspirations of our peoples.

Among the obstacles this ambitious project faced were, **first,** the lack of systematic focus to the research underway and **second,** the difficulty in finding published studies on the subject. Most analysis of Latino religion was in fact not about "Latinos" but about one or other of the several groups. Most of us were in an academic *cul de sac,* wherein Chicanos studied Chicanos while Puerto Ricans studied Puerto Ricans, or Catholics researched Catholicism and Methodists reviewed Methodism, and so on. This fragmentation was multiplied by regional insularity and general indifference to the topic of Latino religion within academia. Individual scholars seldom found colleagues qualified to critically assess their work. To perpetuate the fracturing of Latino religion into its component parts: New York or Los Angeles, Chicano or Puerto Rican, Catholic or Pentecostal did not offer a solution to the problem of disconnectedness. It seemed that only by studying all Latinos and all religions within a comparative framework could PARAL hope to assemble a critical mass of scholars in order to make the dream of a sub-field into a reality.

One key issue that had to be addressed to the satisfaction of social science was whether such a thing as a Latino/Hispanic reality exists or if it was only part of an abstract classificatory system. Does the demographic device of lumping together Spanish-speaking, Latin American born, Spanish-surnamed and Latin American origin peoples translate into a sense of belonging to a nationality? Although many of the bibliographical entries use "Latino," is there such a thing as a Latino group, or is this a misnomer for Mexican Americans, Mexicans, Chicanos, Puerto Ricans, Cuban Americans, etc.? The Latino National Political Survey of 1990 (LNPS) found that respondents preferred the specific nationality name to a general designation like Latino or Hispanic, and it would be presumptive, therefore, to suggest that the majority of Latinos have discarded their nationalities to become members of a new transnationality grouping.

PARAL has always recognized that although the terminology of "Latino" (or "Hispanic") approaches a level of abstraction, it constitutes a viable cultural identity. Latinos are connected to each other by a language, history and worldview that makes us more like each other than like Euro-American groups such as Germans, Poles or the Irish. One should not place the particular national identity into direct competition with a Latino labeling anymore than one places "New Yorker" or "Californian" as a competing identity for "American." Rather than a formula for conformity, "Latino" becomes a rubric for comparative study, uncovering as many contrasts as similarities. The term provides a frame of reference for outlining an ethos or a worldview rather than a substitute for nationality. It may be that "Latino" can be compared to the cultural sense of "Jewish." Even when they do not practice the religion, people of Polish, Russian, German, American and many other national origins claim a commonality as Jews because they experience a common worldview that transcends but does not contradict nationality identities. Latinos also may come to be viewed as a group of disparate nationalities in the United States who share a culture that overlaps with religion.

In any case, the term "Latino" has acquired a real organizational and political meaning. Based on the old saying that "in unity there is strength," during the 1970s and 1980s Chicano, Puerto Rican and other church leaders of the Latino resurgence learned to work together nationally as Latinos, while not surrendering their regional and particular interests. Many of the churches in the United States have established national boards, commissions or divisions to coordinate ministry towards Latinos. Despite limitations imposed by institutional concerns, the churches generally have been more effective in fostering Latino unity at a grassroots level during the past thirty years than many university, political or educational agencies. Parishes and congregations have utilized "Latino" (and "Hispanic") as an ecumenical term, uniting diverse nationality groups in worship and they have done so among large numbers of people across the nation.

Just as corporate America now emphasizes Latino marketing, the various churches are going to have to work harder to enlist or keep Latino members. It would seem that earning the loyalties of Latinos will require churches to approach Latinos in terms of our particularized cultural and spiritual experiences rather than from the posture of a take- it-or-leave-it assimilation. This is why PARAL has chosen to structure its analysis of Latino religion around three key concepts: **syncretism, popular religiosity** and **cultural identity.** These are facets of Latino religious experience that differentiate us from most other believers in the United States. They become the measuring rods with which response to Latino particularities can be evaluated.

An analytical approach to syncretism and religious faith

Without pretending to settle the perpetually vexing question of definition, PARAL asked its scholars to address syncretism with a common premise: "Syncretism is a meshing within a single religious expression of symbols and meanings that originated in distinct credal systems." The idea was to focus upon instances such as the Mexican devotion to Our Lady of Guadalupe where a Christian representation (Mary) acquired religious symbols from native religion (the Aztec maternity cord) or where a single symbol (Santiago, i.e. St. James) has both a Christian meaning (Patron of Spanish cavalry) and an indigenous one (the African Shango or the Peruvian Illapa). Because the historical and anthropological literature has already provided some descriptions of the origins of these fused symbols and meanings, PARAL encouraged a probe into class, racial and economic forces that converge in religious experience.

The literature on syncretism is better developed for Latin America than for Latinos in the United States. It was part of the effort of PARAL to comb studies of syncretism in Latin America for notions that would be applicable to conditions in the United States, and at the same time to outline the particularities of Latino experience. From this analysis have come three premises: **first,** that syncretism is a form of ecumenism that takes place virtually everytime different religious systems come into contact; **second,** syncretism is discriminating, absorbing some elements while rejecting others; and **third,** that the word "syncretism" has a negative connotation.

In order to explain the ubiquity of syncretism to all religion, and not just the Latino experience, we can use comparative analysis to examine the Feast of Passover. The ancient Hebrew rituals served a function similar to the religious expressions common to other peoples who shared the socio-economic reality of the region. The sprinkling of lamb's blood in sacrifice was a common form of thanksgiving for the fertility of the flocks among pastoral nomadic peoples. The baking of unleavened bread took place after the harvest of winter grain, which was baked without the old grain, i.e. yeast. Like the blood sacrifice for nomadic peoples, it was a custom found among other agricultural societies in the region. The special genius of the emerging Hebrew religion was to combine the two rituals in the same seasonal feast. This had the effect of binding together *(re-ligare)* two economic constituencies in a common belief. Thus, at the very beginning of the Judeo-Christian heritage, syncretism took symbols with meaning related to basic rituals of pastoral and agricultural groups and achieved a synthesis with new social, political and religious implications.

Stimulated by extensive contact with Babylon and Egypt, the Hebrews developed a code of laws that provided an awakening sense of nationhood. While they absorbed elements from neighboring religions, and perhaps passed on some of their beliefs in exchange, the Hebrews put limits upon syncretism. From the time of Moses, the pastoral-agricultural ritual of Passover became a mode of recalling that Hebrew origins were different from those of the Egyptians about them. Then, in a return to their homeland, the Passover ritual celebrated the historical moment in which the people separated themselves from Egyptian domination and acquired the meanings of Hebrew nationhood. The early rites of lamb's blood and unleavened bread added a level of meaning that transcended local economic conditions and the cyclical sense of time that had been sufficient for the needs of tribal organization in an earlier Hebrew society.

Syncretism of symbols and religious meaning usually appears after contact with other religions. More importantly, syncretism often lies at the heart of religion's transformations. While theologians emphasize the salvation aspects of this history, social science traces the political, cultural and social components of change in religion. The process of combining social forces into a new religious configuration intensified for the Hebrews with the establishment of a kingdom that sought from the Hebrew faith the legitimation other monarchies derived from their religions. Saul, David, Solomon and their successors imported the trappings of other state religions into Israel. Much of the history in the Book of Kings becomes a struggle between those who want to continue absorbing elements from other religions and societies, and those who refuse to "be like other nations."

This explains the discriminating side of syncretism. We cannot be satisfied with describing the accretions produced by syncretism, but must also be prepared to explain when and why some elements are excluded. Reaction against syncretism contributes as much to the development of religion as continuing to syncretize. Rejection reaffirms one's own traditions and strengthens religious solidarity. Social science analysis needs to show both sides of the process. Properly applied, the study of syncretism restrains social science from reducing all religion to a conditioned reaction to material forces, because the theological responses of rejection must be analyzed as well. For example, the kingdoms of Israel and Judah never fully succeeded in subordinating religion to political and national purposes. In fact, the theological and religious institutions outlasted the kingdoms. With Jerusalem and the temple in ruins and the monarchy shattered, the faith of Israel endured and transformed itself from a state religion into something more. Passover eventually became deliverance from exile in Babylon and the symbol of religious power over political might and earthly dominion. The symbol and meaning of Passover were universalized for subsequent generations of Jews to elaborate for their own needs. Philo explained Passover in terms of Hellenist Platonism and in medieval Spain, Maimonides bent Aristotle to the same purpose. Down to our own day, Passover symbolizes deliverance from continuing oppression of Jewish people everywhere.

Christianity added still another level of meaning to the Jewish Passover rite by making it a recollection of the death of Jesus Christ and a sacrament of the Christian faith. Without denying the existence of the earlier, more limited meaning of the ancient Hebrew spring rituals or their applications to the establishment of a Jewish nation, the focus was placed upon the abstract concept of deliverance from sinfulness, i.e. redemption. Bread and wine were preserved as symbols of thanksgiving for food, but the same symbols also became Christ's body and blood in order to recall his martyrdom among Christians much as the Passover rite reminded Jewish believers of deliverance under Moses.

Passover is hardly the only example of the connections between syncretism and the development of the Judeo-Christian religious faith. The alternating pattern of accepting and rejecting syncretism helps explain why the clashes between Hellenists and Judaizers led to early rifts in the apostolic church. Syncretism underlies the encounter with Roman religion and—after the fifth century—with the beliefs of the invading Germanic peoples. Throughout the Post-Constantinian and medieval periods, aspects of existing religious systems were given a level of meaning that coincided with some facet of Christianity. For instance, the functions of female deities were transferred to Mary and the saints, thus distributing supernatural power along a hierarchical spectrum congruous with Christian theology. Rather than spurn this process, medieval Christians welcomed it. They generally considered this coalescence of different religious traditions to constitute the acceptance of Christianity. In such a religious climate, local religion reflected the myriad strands of original beliefs, all textured into the fabric of a church that celebrated virtually every manifestation of the sacred. Not that medieval Christianity lacked discernment towards limiting syncretism, since most religious movements—including heretical ones—advocated new sets of boundaries for the faith. But even the periodic efforts at centralizing and controlling the medieval tolerance could not replace the syncretistic practice of combining old beliefs with Christian forms while evangelizing. The mindset was carried across the Atlantic to the Indies in the fifteenth and early sixteenth centuries, and the earliest missionary efforts in the Americas reflect a thousand year old policy of Christian conversion via syncretism.

The Reformation, however, rejected many medieval expressions of faith. In the desire to return to a simpler, more biblical Christianity, syncretism came to be viewed as a contamination of the Gospel. But the discrimination against syncretism during the Reformation adopted biblical norms **as these were culturally understood.** While Protestant theology can be studied as something new, the rejection of syncretistic elements was just another example in the long Christian history of the alternating currents between attraction and rejection of syncretism. Moreover, one sees variance within Protestantism regarding how much syncretism was to be rejected. Thus, for instance, while Martin Luther rejected the cult of the saints, he celebrated Christmas with evergreen trees borrowed from the symbolism of ancient German beliefs. John Calvin rejected devotion to the saints but also recommended that the folly of Christmas celebration be studiously avoided because the observance of Christ's birthday on December 25th and the use of holly were importations from Roman religious rituals for the winter solstice.

Viewing the Reformation from the perspective of syncretism moves social science analysis towards consideration of the theological process itself. How did class, education and national origin influence both Luther and Calvin? Does conflict theory relate Calvin's rejection of age old Christmas celebrations to the way new groups reinforce their identity as distinct from others around them? How did Luther's affection for traditional German Christmas customs affect the peasant following of early Lutheranism? And how can we explain Calvin's rejection of the rituals of Ash Wednesday—which have a solid foundation in the religion of Ancient Israel—as a restoration of biblical religion?

These considerations about two reformers make the point, I think, that syncretism must be considered in virtually every change in religious expression. Even when the inclusion of elements borrowed from other religions is overtly rejected on theological grounds, the rejection can be analyzed. Social science will find that religion sometimes opts for action and belief against its best interests, and that theology does not always obey the predictable laws of self or class interest. But elucidating this dissonance is as important to the study of religion as explaining the material factors that cause syncretism. The two processes make religion work, much like an electrical current needs to alternate positive and negative charges in the flow to keep the motors running. Syncretistic innovation is balanced with tradition, helping a religion change without losing its particular identity. An American style Christmas with a Christmas tree taken from barbarian religion, mistletoe from the Druids and holly from the Roman Saturnalia, is nonetheless a Christian holiday. These syncretistic elements have been successfully incorporated in forms that are theologically acceptable to most of the U.S. churches. In a sense, as the tale of Tiny Tim and Ebenezer Scrooge reminds us, the religious meaning of Christmas is wrapped up in a package made of syncretism, and those who say "Humbug!" to the sycretistic elements are likely to forget the religious meaning as well.

Robert Wuthnow suggests in his foreword to this volume that syncretism is underway in a host of disguises within American religion and not just among Latinos. He describes as syncretism the practice of a Methodist minister in Indiana who wears a yarmulke in his services. Here again, syncretistic innovation is a motor of change and a bridge to relevance. But the Indiana minister has not confused Methodism and Judaism. His theological discernment makes his expression of syncretism a tolerant appreciation of another religion's beliefs rather than a surrender of his own.

Syncretism in Latino religion has to be viewed similarly. The inclusion of vestiges of Aztec religion within a Marian devotion among Latinos, for instance, is a process not very different from the one that has given the United States its Christmas time symbols. It may be necessary to discuss with greater clarity how there is a discriminating facet to Latino syncretism, just as there has been for other types of religion in the United States. But the point has been made, I think, that syncretism is a widespread phenomenon and not just a quirk of Latino religion.

But if syncretism frequently occurs in America's religions, why is the term "syncretism" so seldom applied to the Euro-American experiences, and often used pejoratively for Latinos? One dimension that must be woven into the analysis of contemporary syncretism, I think, is that of ethnocentric amnesia. Latinos today are no more likely conscious of Aztec syncretism in our traditions than British Protestants are of borrowings from the Roman *lares,* Germanic barbarians and the Druids. Paraphrasing Lord Berkeley, "If we have forgotten that a tradition was derived from syncretism, does syncretism still exist?" Analysis of the interaction of different credal symbols in Latino traditions should be compared with the same process in other cultural forms of American religion, wherein the intention is to be Christian not syncretistic.

This does not mean, however, that syncretism for Latinos has no differences from more generalized religious experiences in the United States. In *Enigmatic Powers,* the third volume of the series, it was suggested that syncretism is a "place" rather than a thing. Along with other cogent observations, this nudges us into viewing syncretism as a politicized religious process, very much related to social location. One reason syncretism is more noticed in Latino religion than in Euro-American religion may be connected to social class. Preoccupation with upward mobility often inhibits syncretism because its expression is identified with less educated, less assimilated segments of society. Much of Euro-American religion today, both Protestant and Catholic, seems to eschew customs rooted in ethnic practice because these are viewed as vestiges of a now abandoned lower class identity. In contrast, Latino religion embraces these customs as a constituent part of its essence. One finds in all three PARAL volumes the insistence that Latinos need to preserve these native customs which echo indigenous religions because this is a measure of authenticity. As will be discussed below in connection with popular religion, Latino religion views itself as the experience of a population that is economically deprived and the embrace of syncretistic elements is part of this identity.

The problem with continuing to describe such aspects of Latino religion by linking them with syncretism is the heavy baggage the term has accumulated. Clearly, racial attitudes have a significant influence in categorizing as "syncretism" Christian experience with indigenous American religion or African religion. Christian expression influenced by contact with non-European beliefs is often seen as somehow inferior. In the inescapable formulation of Otto Maduro, those who hold power use their control of the modes of religious production to serve the interests of their class and race. Religion, whether in Latin America or in the United States, historically reflects the social divisions of class and race, with a lamentable segregation of the rich and mostly white from the poor who often are of color. As in Latin American societies, race in the United States is a notion that smuggles in social class categorization. The term "syncretism" (or "folk") in reference to Latino religion feeds the perception that our faith is localized in racial and social inferiority. Crudely expressed, this enables a label of "syncretism" for anything connected to non-white religious groups, as if the true and pure faith has been contaminated. Among the rest of the population, however, the same phenomenon is viewed as a reasonable form of accommodation to changing circumstances.

It would appear that the majority of scholars in PARAL have concluded that because syncretism is unfairly lumped with magic, superstition and racist inferiorization, using this term to describe Latino religion is problematic. This is not to say that analysis of Latino religion should run away from race and class considerations: only that such research is unnecessarily penalized by using confusing terminology. If a new concept is intended, it would be better to use a new term rather than be stuck with "syncretism." Achieving wide acceptance for a replacement, however, will not be an easy task. Indeed, although PARAL scholars are clearly pointing to a new terminology, the social science literature on syncretism in this bibliography frequently echoes the negative conceptualizations described above.

Finally, the syncretistic process in Latino religion is not limited to centuries old contact with Meso-American religions. Santería, the Afro-Cuban religion, is growing today and not only among Latinos. In most instances, as Andrés Pérez y Mena insists, it **complements** rather than **competes** with Catholicism. Along with New Age beliefs that borrow from Native American religious concepts, Afro-Cuban religion seems to have found a niche within Catholicism. As such, both fill a vacuum in today's Latino religion, much as Methodism and later Pentecostalism remedied a dour Predestinationism by adding the sweet emotion of God's amazing grace.

Afro-Cuban religion in particular finds God's power in sensuality, an element of the sacred fairly common in the world's religions. A sacral sensuality is essential to a human experience of religion, even if the Judeo-Christian tradition has generally avoided this kind of openness about the body. Afro-Cuban religion rushes in to occupy the vacuum left by an official Christianity that seems paralyzed by body consciousness. Its syncretism compensates for something that is lacking to Catholicism. In a similar way, Native American traditions of healing seem to have filled a vacuum in the linkage between faith and good health. (One might ask to what extent faiths based on healing, such as Christian Scientism and Seventh Day Adventism, fit into this pattern of void filling).

In sum, syncretism in Latino religion is a topic that needs new terminology and a revised theoretical approach. Its proper analysis demands attention not only to material influences, but a readiness to examine theological boundary-setting on religious terms. Race and class, tradition and change are notions that have to be incorporated into a comparative framework that includes not only the expressions of Latino religion, but experiences taken from other American religions as well.

Appropriating popular religiosity as a distinctive characteristic

Scholarly discourse sometimes connects the term "syncretism" with "popular religion." PARAL sees the two as related: cause to effect, process to result. But in Spain and Latin America, the term "popular religion" has been replaced by *"religiosidad popular."* In a somewhat Solomonic decision, we chose in this series to use the term, "popular religiosity," rather than "popular religion." Our working definition of popular religiosity was "the subjective disposition of people to innovate, develop and celebrate religious expression without clerical or institutional control." With this decision, we hoped to place discussion of the symbol content of belief under syncretism, leaving intentionality to the examination of popular religiosity.

This pragmatic approach focused the analysis in *An Enduring Flame* so that each of the authors could develop ideas that echoed those of their colleagues. By emphasizing the subjective disposition over the content of the belief or practice, we placed traditions like Marian processions on the same footing with Aztec sacred dances. This was not because we were blind to the theological differences between these distinct customs, but because Latino believers bring the same kind of attitudes towards both and our focus was upon the people's lived religious experience. In order to study the role of other factors in shaping popular religiosity, the first step required each belief to be treated as equally valid within a social science perspective.

But analyzing popular religiosity in this comparative framework produced several unanticipated problems. The first concerned theology. Most Latino theologians in the United States, especially those from the Catholic tradition, have identified popular religiosity as the distinctive characteristic of Latino Catholicism.[7] Their definitions and approaches do not always complement the social science perspective of the PARAL enterprise. For instance, besides often ignoring the rich traditions of African-American religion, Latino Catholic theologians give scant consideration of popular religiosity among Euro-American Catholics such as Italians, Germans and Poles. These other religiosities may differ from those among Latinos, but without comparative study it is hard to distinguish what belongs to "**Latino** popular religiosity" and what is simply "popular religiosity."

Secondly, the anti-clerical agenda that Robert Wuthnow described in the foreword bubbles to the surface in much of this current theology. The opposite of "popular religiosity" Is not "unpopular religiosity" but "clerically controlled religiosity." Theologians argue among themselves whose definition of popular religiosity is closer to the people's sense. Some argue that clerical control is usually benign and others that it is essentially antagonistic towards the people's interests.[8] The scholars of PARAL found "control" to be a very slippery term indeed, and there appears to be no rule for determining it. Moreover, the clergy are not the only ones to attempt control of popular religiosity. The ethnic revivals among Latinos have produced a cottage industry of folk cultural festivals. Much like the shopper who finds that the authentic Pueblo Indian art for sale in the mall was mass produced in Malaysia, the scholar may find some expressions of Latino popular religiosity are commercialized imitations sponsored by merchants interested in businesses like selling beer to a festival's onlookers.

We have to turn on the blinking amber light of caution. While there is an advantage to staking out a special claim for Latino popular religiosity, there are also dangers. Assuredly, popular religiosity—

even if it is found among other believers—has been preserved in unique ways by Latinos today, perhaps as a result of our non-immigrant circumstance. But popular religiosity is not always liberating or ennobling, in fact it sometimes perpetuates stereotypes in gender and social relations that impede increased community awareness. Social science must tread carefully so as not to fall into the trap of distorting popular religiosity by romanticizing it.

Popular religiosity is best viewed not as an idealized notion but rather than as a people's lived experience. Approached this way, popular religiosity emerges as an historical factor in Iberian influenced Christianity and not as the target of today's romantization. A more detailed examination of popular Catholicism's roots in fourteenth century Iberian traditions would help trace Latino popular religiosity to medieval *cofradías*. The *cofradías* built their own churches, hired and fired chaplains, and assumed important civic functions. Each of these organizations had a monopoly over any public manifestation of devotion to a particular saint. Run by lay people, the *cofradías* were financed by a system of membership fees, interest from insurance funds, and often indulged in a rank commercialism of selling religious articles and managing pilgrimages. These secular forces limited the faith content of popular religiosity, much as theology limited syncretism.

Some of today's Latino lay societies in both Catholicism and Protestantism exercise a communitarian and civic influence comparable to that enjoyed by the medieval *cofradías*. In Santería too, we find that many *casas* operate with the same mixture of religious belonging and commercial profit from spiritual need.[9] This should not be surprising since these structures of the Afro-Cuban religion derive from the *cabildos* in Spanish colonial Cuba, which were organized to serve the African slaves, much as the *cofradías* had done for the white population in Europe. Social science research into Latino popular religiosity would benefit from a closer historical review of these medieval institutions in order to better understand contemporary practice.

The third, and perhaps most daunting challenge presented by the theological literature concerns the relationship of popular religiosity to belief. While social science can compare different customs and analyze the nature and extent of control of popular religiosity by the elites, questions of faith content ought to be settled by theologians. Rather than a solution, this option presents greater difficulties to social science research. Theologians dispute among themselves the value of the faith expressed in popular religiosity. On the one hand, we are told that Latino popular religiosity is equivalent to the theological notion of *sensus fidelium*—the sense of the faithful. In this concept, the belief of the lay people has a role in the interpretation of the faith. What the people have believed, some say, is a criterion for establishing doctrine.[10] Carried to its logical (but probably unintended) conclusion, this would mean that issues like birth control could be settled by polling the "faithful" for their belief. But on the other hand, it has been declared that Mexican natives would not have had "the thought patterns or the worldview" necessary for understanding the doctrine of the trinity "until they were Europeanized."[11] (One wonders if the same could be said of Germanic barbarians in the fourth century, and if so, then belief in trinitarian monotheism would have been against the *sensus fidelium* for about half a millennium of the Christian experience!) How is social science to interpret these divergent assessments of the theological importance of popular religiosity, especially when the theologians' judgments are based upon some non-theological statements about mental capacity? This problem is not very different from questionable psychological judgments made about the capacity for religious faith by non-theologians such as Ramón Gutierrez in his book, *When Jesus Came, the Corn Mothers Went Away.*

In contrast to what might become an inquisitorial mindset, the theologians, two Catholics and one Protestant, writing in *An Enduring Flame* adopt a common sense approach to the issue of whether or not popular religiosity is true faith. They simply take people at their word. If the native says that the feminine form arrayed in ornaments common to the Aztec corn goddess is Mary, the Mother of God, then that stated belief is the belief of the people.[12] There is no recourse to subtext readings or psychological analyses of the believers. Without dismissing the insightfulness of the deconstructionist approach to certain facets of religious expression, this common sense decision about faith has much to recommend it. Nonetheless, the reader should be alerted that differing perspectives will be found in many of the entries in the bibliography.

Several articles in *An Enduring Flame* suggest that gender roles have important functions in popular religiosity.[13] Perhaps because it is removed from a clerical culture, Latino popular religiosity celebrates masculinity and femininity in intriguing ways. As Ana María Díaz-

Stevens suggests, there seems to be a "matriarchal core" to popular religiosity that elevates women in religious society. One must be attentive to nuance of gender in ritual agents and symbols to fully understand the importance popular religiosity exercises among Latinos. In a similar vein, Richard Flores's careful description of the troupe performing La Pastorela in San Antonio shows the value of subtlety in time and space. The performers know when their representation of the Christmas story is for show and when it is for God. The same play changes from performance to devotion by uncontrolled circumstances that require spontaneity and coincidence to gain sacralizing power. There is a hint here of Max Weber's notion of charismatic religion. In this case, however, it is not a single leader but the community that acquires the charismatic moment.

For Weber, the opposite of charismatic religion was the routinization of faith. At first blush, some exercises of popular religiosity such as the recitation of the rosary at a wake, would seem to be a prime example of routinization rather than of charismatic religion. But by adding the dimensions of time, space, gender and other local elements to the subject of analysis, the unique and charismatic characteristics of popular religiosity emerge. It may be that what is most important in the recitation of the rosary is the affirmation by kin and friends of a common responsibility that can only be fully realized by actually attending the wake. Thus, contact with the sacred for believers comes from the unique emotional content of practicing a communal everyday ritual at a special time and under special circumstances. To repeat an analogy from *An Enduring Flame*, religious feeling is the flame, while the ritual is the candle that is lighted. The candle is visible and present, even when not lighted, but only fulfills its function when the flame is burning.

Analyzing popular religiosity as a collective charisma may also help address the issue of whether or not Latino Pentecostals and Evangelical Christians have a popular religiosity. As pointed out in *An Enduring Flame*, the first Protestant missionaries among Latinos generally saw it their duty to eliminate popular Catholicism and the religiosity it nourished.[14] But these efforts were largely directed at the **form** rather than the **feeling** of the people as they approached the sacred. Could it be that the direct access to the Holy Spirit and the window upon the miraculous offered by Pentecostal worship is the same as popular Catholicism's search for contact with God? This would place Latino popular religiosity in both Pentecostalism and Catholicism as similar feelings with different ritual forms: two differently shaped candles lighted from the same match, as it were. It might also be necessary to use the term "Pentecostalistic" rather than "Pentecostalism" in this context because there is ample evidence that the Pentecostal forms of prayer flourish within Catholicism and Evangelical Protestantism. One need not belong to a church of Pentecostalism to utilize Pentecostalistic religiosity.

The relationship of Pentecostal and Evangelical religion to a long-standing Catholic culture is very much discussed today in studies of Latin America. Not all of these studies are directly applicable to the Latino experience in the United States, however, since in this country Protestants are dominant and Catholics are the minority, the exact reverse of Latin America. But as a departure point for further analysis into the Latino reality, this literature on conversions to Protestantism and Pentecostalism in Latin America needs to be reviewed.

Latino cultural Identity as religious belonging

Denominational membership is the most familiar ground for social science research on Latino religion to date. In *Old Masks, New Faces*, Gilbert R. Cadena reviewed the data available demonstrating that virtually every existing survey of Latino religion includes questions about denominational membership. On the basis of such data, conclusions have been drawn on matters as divergent as voting patterns and the frequency of bible reading. But although such correlations are easy pickings for mainstream social science, we need to beware of the trap of merely repeating quantitative data as if it were a replacement for more sensitive qualitative insight.

Many of the values that are considered properties of Latino culture have a birth certificate from religion. The oft-repeated notion of Latino family values, for instance, frequently speaks of reverence for elders and the practice of *compadrazgo*. These are traditions which are traceable to religious customs that over time have been merged into a general cultural template. In this sense, the warmth of emotion, the love of *fiesta*, the sense of destiny and a host of other "Latino cultural characteristics" are derived from a religious worldview. Even when a Latino no longer practices a faith, this mindset endures. Often one is not considered to possess a Latino culture unless there is some expression of these values, even if they are divorced from religious observance. As has been alluded to in the opening part of this essay, it can be asked if Latinos are creating a transnational cultural identity for themselves, much as Jews have already done.

The volume of the PARAL series, *Old Masks, New Faces* helped formulate several additional issues to be addressed in the analysis of how Latino cultural identity is related to religion. The first concerns social class. While most Latinos are poor by the standards of socio-economic analysis, Latino culture cannot be reduced to a culture of poverty. Some of those who celebrate Latino street culture run this risk of identifying the particular circumstance of poverty with all Latino experience. It is a difficult and narrow line to walk in the analysis of Latino religion. Clearly, Latino religion is practiced among the nation's poorest groups. But while many of our churches help people cope with drug addiction, spousal abuse or violent street crime, that is not the only definition of Latino religion, because we had Latino religion even before these situations became widespread.

In a similar vein, the dichotomous categories of "we" - "they" for cultural behavior can lead us into confusion. Like so many others, I have utilized a contrast between Latino communal thinking and Anglo individualism as an explanatory device for cultural differences. But ideal types can easily become stereotypes that reduce reality to rigid categorization. It seems to me that there are better ways to describe cultural patterns than to rely on dichotomous types.[15] A national survey is necessary to understand Latino identity, but it will be effective only if it incorporates the kind of nuances that have been elaborated in the PARAL research.

Social identity, however, always unfolds by interaction with institutions. We need to examine Latino membership in the several churches against the background of denominationalism in U.S. religion. Until recently, there has been a remarkable parallelism in American Protestantism between social position and denominational affiliation. But the changing faces of population in urban neighborhoods have substituted racial minorities for Euro-Americans to such a degree that some congregations must recruit minorities as members or else face closure. With African Americans, Protestantism has a long tradition of incorporating black membership and clergy. But with Latinos, the Protestant churches are faced with a particular challenge that approximates creation *ex nihilo*.

Despite the presence of Latinos who have been Protestant over several generations, the greatest increase in Latino membership in Evangelical and Pentecostal churches today appears to come by personal conversion. In large measure, Latinos have not passed through a historical process of raising their class status to correspond to religious affiliation in the ranking that was once generally applicable to U. S. Protestantism. (I suspect that the Asian presence in the United States has intensified this transformation, but that is another story.) As we enter the 21st century, Latinos provide a catalyst to complete the transformation of the social location of most Protestant denominations. Geography, that is, proximity to a particular church, may be more of a factor in Latino membership than a similarity in social class with other members of the denomination.

The changing nature of Protestant denominationalism makes it perplexing that a respected Catholic theologian recently analyzed Latino conversion to evangelical and Pentecostal denominations as "a search for modernity" by utilizing the interpretation of George M. Marsden that Protestantism is "modern" on account of its individualism and the privatization of religion.[16] The idea is launched that because of its traditional, communitarian values Catholicism is losing Latinos who aspire to upward mobility in a secular society and therefore choose to become Protestants.

Some facts argue otherwise. Analysis of data from the 1991 CUNY survey of religious affiliation, for instance, shows that women church members had higher rates of educational attainment than the general female population. The exceptions were women who belonged to Protestant denominations such as the Baptists and Pentecostals.[17] Now if female educational attainment is a key value of modernity, then many Baptists and Pentecostals are not "modern" on this score. The same survey showed that with 7%, Baptists had the highest number of Latino adherents to Protestantism, while 3% of all Latino believers were Pentecostals. Based on this data and similar findings in other sources, I would argue that a majority of Latinos who convert to Protestantism and Pentecostalism choose denominations that **do not** seek modernity. In this instance as in so many others, survey data along with ethnography are preferable to an over reliance on ideal type theories in explaining complex religious processes.

The sea changes underway in Protestant denominationalism can be applied to the Catholic tradition also. In the United States, ethnic groupings within Catholicism often differentiate social class location much as Protestant denominationalism. The chief vehicle for ethnic segregation within U.S. Catholicism has been the national parish. This is a local church that defines its members by language use. The national parishes of U.S. Catholicism were intended to serve particular ethnic groups only until English was learned. Cultural and linguistic assimilation, however, paralleled upward social mobility. The general expectation has been that second or third generation Italians, for instance, would be less tied to the Italian language and culture than their parents, but also richer and better educated. And while there has been some reconsideration about the role of these national parishes in assimilating Catholic ethnic groups into U.S. society, the members of an ethnic national parish were usually perceived as lower in social class than the parishioners of an English-speaking territorial parish, somewhat the way Baptists have been viewed in comparison with Episcopalians.

Euro-American national parishes were disappearing in the 1940s when, in the face of a growing migration of Mexican Americans from Texas to Chicago and of Puerto Ricans to New York, the U.S. Catholic bishops undertook a major pastoral initiative. Catholicism in these major urban archdioceses established offices for the Spanish-speaking to help replace the Euro-American population which had begun to move to U.S. suburbs during the 1950s. Territorial parishes began to provide services in the Spanish language, thus blurring the older distinction between the territorial and the national parishes. The Spanish-speaking and the English-speaking belonged to the same parish and used the same buildings, but now sermons, hymns, catechism and the sacraments were also available in Spanish. In effect, the churches became bilingual—using two languages to translate the same Latin rites and dogmas into Spanish as well as into English.

Within two decades, this strategy had gained wide acceptance in Catholicism. But in the mid-1960s, the II Vatican Council initiated its sweeping reforms. The U.S. Catholic church was obliged to replace the Tridentine Latin mass with a liturgy in the language of the people. It could no longer be argued, as it once was, that Latin—which virtually no one understood—unified all Catholics. Now intelligibility, participation and creative expressiveness were measures of Catholic practice. A sea change had occurred, in which bilingualism, i. e. speaking two languages, had become multiculturalism, i. e. using different languages as a mode of expressing different cultures.

The multiculturalism produced by the conciliar reforms allowed Latino Catholicism to view itself not as a Spanish language version of the same U.S. Catholicism, but as the flowering of a different cultural tradition that had roots different from those of the English-speaking congregations. Stimulated by a plethora of lay Catholic organizations and movements, Latino Catholic practice became an **alternative** to, rather than a **copy** of, the rest of U.S. Catholicism. Ana María Díaz-Stevens suggests that because Latinos had been used to a Catholicism with minimal clerical presence, we can be considered a model for what the U.S. Catholic church will become as a priestless Catholicism is forced upon the national institution.[18] The concept of a "cultural Catholic" which Andrew Greeley introduced in the 1970s as a wave of the future for Euro-American Catholics, appears a great deal like an experience 400 years old among Latinos, wherein lay people manage religious practice with minimal influence from clerical elites. Self-starting lay leadership also explains the great interest scholars of Latino religion have in the notion of "organic leadership" as developed by Antonio Gramsci.

Blurred loyalties in denominational belonging can be found not only among the laity, but also within clerical ranks. Catholic and Protestant Latino clergy, as well as an increasing number of Pentecostal leaders cooperate in various community initiatives. Reliance on the same pastoral and theological works, heightened interest in preserving Latino culture, and frequent dialogue about social and neighborhood problems, have moved Latinos towards ecumenism. But this is ecumenism with a twist. Latino affinities are with each other on the basis of religious culture rather than through the institution. In other words, Latino Catholics may feel themselves closer to Latino Methodists than to non-Latino Catholics because the experience of community is based on culture, not on denominational loyalty or theology.

PARAL has conducted its research against this backdrop. In the light of substantial changes in the meaning of Protestant denominationalism and ethnic Catholicism, current explanations for Latino religious identification require review. Nor are Latinos the only persons who can contribute to this scholarship. Granted that those who have experienced Latino religion as their heritage bring certain insights to research, but ideas are not generated by nationality. While we seek what is particular to Latinos, we need also compare the religious experience of others with our own. At a time when more than one commentator has analyzed the "vanishing boundaries" in American religion, the Latino case offers new areas for research for every scholar committed to the truth.

Conclusion

I trust that this essay will serve as a map through the four volumes of the PARAL series and many of the works which have made a contribution to general knowledge of the field. Clearly, the task of discovering Latino religion is very much a work in progress. Latino religion cannot be approached as an afterthought to theory on religion in America. Still less can Latino religion be reduced to an area study of an immigrant group on the way to assimilation. Moreover, as a social science field which is still emerging, the study of Latino religion can contribute towards changing society. No less than theologians and pastoral ministers, members of the academy can make contributions to the betterment of society. As the Puerto Rican born Eugenio María de Hostos, Citizen of the Americas, observed over a hundred years ago, social science is the most moral of all sciences because the study of social interactions implies that we have an obligation to improve. We will be successful in our research when we can say with Hostos that "such an obligation is also the cause and fountain of our happiness."

Endnotes

1. For a detailed explanation of these demographics see Joan Moore, "The Social Fabric of the Hispanic Community since 1965" in Jay P. Dolan and Allan Figueroa Deck, S.J. eds. *Hispanic Catholic Culture in the U.S.: Issues and Concerns,* (University of Notre Dame Press: Notre Dame, 1994) pp. 6-49. Her previous work with Harry Pachón, *Hispanics in the United States,* (Englewood Cliffs: Prentice Hall, 1985) is also quite good, but unfortunately does not contain 1990 census data.

2. To follow the essay style, multiple end notes and citations are held to a minimum here. In a sense, the entire bibliography and the preceding volumes amply serve that function. This essay is intended to serve as a guide to the key issues that undergird most of social science inquiry into Latino religion, and the works of contributing

authors are listed in reference to the volume in which they appear. Unfortunately, at the time of this writing, pagination was not available for all three books.

3. Antonio M. Stevens-Arroyo, *Prophets Denied Honor: An Anthology on the Hispanic Church,* (Maryknoll: Orbis Books, 1980).

4. The term "Hispanic" is appropriate here because some of the bishops were born in Spain. Noteworthy, however, is their identification with Latinos and not with other Euro-Americans.

5. See my article, "The Emergence of a Social Identity among Latino Catholics: An Appraisal," In *Hispanic Catholic Culture in the U.S.,* pp. 77-130.

6. For a fuller description of Pious Colonialism, see my article "Latino Catholicism and the Eye of the Beholder: Notes Towards a New Sociological Paradigm," in *Latino Studies Journal* 6:2 (May 1995) 22-25.

7. This theme is common among the contributors to Allan Figueroa Deck, S.J, ed., *Frontiers of Hispanic Catholic Theology in the United States,* (Maryknoll: Orbis Books, 1992), Justo L. González, ed., *Voces: Voices From the Hispanic Church* (Nashville: Abingdom, 1992) and Roberto S. Goizueta, editor, *We Are a People!* (Minneapolis: Fortress Press, 1992). See also Figueroa Deck's summary "Latino Theology: The Year of the Boom" in *Journal of Hispanic/Latino Theology* 1:2 (February 1994) p. 57 *et passim.*

8. Robert E. Wright, "If It's Official, It Can't Be Popular? Reflections on Popular and Folk Religion" *Journal of Hispanic/Latino Theology* 1:3 (May 1994) pp. 47-67, and the counter- arguments by Orlando O. Espín, "Popular Religion as an Epistemology (of Suffering)" 2:2 (November 1994) pp. 55-78, especially pp. 66-67, where he accuses Wright of "dismissing [Latinos]... and their religious universe as ultimately insignificant to theology and society."

9. See Mercedes Cros Sandoval about the Cuban experience and Andrés Pérez y Mena for the adaptation among Puerto Ricans in New York in *Enigmatic Powers.*

10. Orlando O. Espín, "Tradition and Popular Religion: An Understanding of the *Sensus Fidelium*" in *Frontiers of Hispanic Theology,* pp. 62-87.

11. Orlando O. Espín, "Trinitarian Monotheism and the Birth of Popular Catholicism: The Case of Sixteenth Century Mexico" *Missiology* 20:2 (1992), page 179.

12. In *An Enduring Flame*, Puerto Rican Jaime Vidal addresses this issue directly, but his approach is echoed in Virgilio Elizondo's descriptions of the Mexican American experience. Luis Rivera Pagán, the Protestant among the three, focuses upon 16th century texts with the same measure of common sense understanding.

13. Ana María Díaz-Stevens and Meredith McGuire point to these roles from the viewpoint of women today: Jaime Vidal and Gustavo Benavides discuss the issue as elements of conceptualizing the sacred.

14. The articles written by Samuel Silva-Gotay of the University of Puerto Rico and Ana María Díaz-Stevens of Union Theological Seminary develop this point.

15. See Caleb Rosado and Edwin Hernández in *Old Masks, New Faces*.

16. Allan Figueroa Deck, S. J. "The Challenge of Evangelical/ Pentecostal Christianity to *Hispanic Catholicism" in Hispanic Catholic Culture in the U.S.*, pp. 409-439.

17. Barry A. Kosmin and Ariela Keysar, "The Impact of Religious Identification on the Education of American Women," *Journal for the Scientific Study of Religion* (forthcoming, Spring 1995).

18. Ana María Díaz-Stevens, *Oxcart Catholicism on Fifth Avenue,* (Notre Dame Press: University of Notre Dame Press, 1993).

A NOTE TO THE USER

Segundo Pantoja

Preparing a bibliography when none existed before was a great challenge. After extensive meetings and discussions with my mentor, Anthony M. Stevens-Arroyo, I was given considerable latitude to fashion a project based on my own considerations and insights.

I compiled this bibliography in three steps. First, I conducted computerized library searches using the facilities of several institutions: Princeton University, Union Theological Seminary, CUNY-Graduate Center, and the New York Public Library.

I searched all major indexes located at the institutions named above for entries that bore on the relation of Latinos to religion. Among them, those which rendered best results were the Chicano Periodical Index, Hispanic American Periodical Index (HAPI), Religion Index, International Dissertation Abstracts, (ATLA) Religion Data Base, Social Sciences Citation Index, Sociofile, and Psychological Abstracts.

I proceeded to elicit items from these indexes by entering subject headings that ranged from the general to the specific, e.g., starting with Hispanics and Religion, Latinos and Religion; then proceeding to look for the specific nationalities, Mexican Americans, Puerto Ricans; and ending with some of the recent immigrant groups such as Dominicans, Colombians, and those from Central America. Of course, most of the time entries in data bases were located under the heading *Hispanics and Religion,* rather than under the nationality headings, and among these the largest share was for the Mexican American and Puerto Rican groups.

But although each of these indexes is valuable, none is complete. They are limited to a set of mainstream journals, while the study of Latino religion has a wider audience and is published more extensively.

This led to the second step in fashioning the bibliography. I drew entries from the *curricula vitae* of both PARAL members and other contributors to the series, on the premise that as leaders in the field, their publications were essential to the bibliography. My third step was to examine the syllabuses prepared for courses taught by PARAL members as well as the reading lists they had compiled for their classes. My thinking was that if a selection was important to them, it was important to PARAL.

I included entries only if the title or abstract indicated that the piece in question dealt with the relationship between Latinos and religion as its main topic, or at least if it touched on such a relationship in a substantial manner. To classify the entries appropriately, the rule of thumb followed was a mix of intuition and either knowledge about the type of publication or about the author. Thus I came up with the two main categories on social science and theological/religious publications. Despite my best efforts, the bibliography cannot completely escape the risk of misclassification of some entries. In any case, the intention was to make the present bibliography user-friendly. For that purpose, it has been organized into four sections. The first two parts are arranged according to the type of publication in which the article appears: the social sciences first, the religious or theological field second. The third section lists documents such as several bibliographies on related subjects, reports, speeches, unpublished conference papers, and important newspaper or magazine articles. Fortunately, many of these are reproduced or excerpted in the 1980 book, *Prophets Denied Honor*. The final section lists theses and dissertations by graduates from both religious and secular institutions.

An apology is in order to all those who have dealt in their writings with the religious experiences of Latinos, but whose work does not appear here. Because I was forced to rely on the title in selecting for the bibliography, I may have missed some works whose titles did not clearly refer to Latino religion. Moreover, I could have omitted relevant writings that were part of more general works.

I also encountered some unsuspected problems in listing entries. For one, some entries were incomplete but I opted for keeping them in until further research allows us to improve the bibliography. Secondly, several women authors have used different names reflecting, no doubt, changes in marital status and today's heightened awareness of yesterday's patriarchal preferences. I felt bound to list the entries as they originally appeared, although I recognize this may lead to some confusion. Style was also an issue, since the social sciences follow one format and theology, one of the humanities, another. All the entries here follow the social science format of the Chicago Manual of Style.

Finally, because of limitations of time, personnel, and direct access to much of the material for which the entries stand, this is not an annotated bibliography. However, PARAL has now launched a newsletter, one of whose features will be to offer abstracts on current works and research on Latino religion. With the continued cooperation of scholars of Latino religion, this will contribute to the data base that this bibliography represents and permit future efforts to include extensive descriptions of more recent publications.

Many persons helped to make this volume possible, and at the risk of regrettably leaving out some of them, I would like to especially thank Jorge Klor de Alva at Princeton University, Seth Kasten and Drew Kadel at Union Theological Seminary, Kenneth G. Davis at Oblate School of Theology. Gilbert R. Cadena at Pomona College and Alberto Pulido at Arizona State University provided me with their bibliography in Chicano Studies.

I hope the reader will be as well served by this bibliography as I have been. Two years ago, when I began as a research assistant in the Program for the Analysis of Religion Among Latinos (PARAL), I was a neophyte in the field of religion. But the task of preparing the bibliography helped me to realize the marvelous diversity of Latinos and of our religious experiences. The entries in the bibliography reflect the efforts over the years and across the land by many to study, comment, and make known-each from their own perspective-the variety of ways in which Latinos and religion touch each other. The reader will realize that most writings are dated within the last thirty years, an indication, on the one hand, that exploration of Latino religiosity is new in relation to the already old Latino experience in the U.S. and, on other hand, that interest has been surging as Latinos grow in numbers and diversity.

I am glad that I am participating in the emergence of Latino religion in the United States. Mine has been the good fortune as a sociology graduate student of participating in the ground-breaking work of PARAL. It has been a process made easier and warm by the company and guidance of Anthony Stevens-Arroyo and Ana María Díaz-Stevens as well as other PARAL members. Thanks to my involvement with PARAL, I came to discover other facets of myself: A latent religiosity lying underneath layers of learned academic rationality, and a heightened sense of ethnicity as I feel that every day that goes by I am less of an immigrant from Latin America and I become more of a Latino. I see myself setting down roots here, especially after the birth of Oriana, my daughter, a New Yorker with Colombian and Dominican extended families and, of course, a Latina!

Social Science Publications

I

Abalos, David T. 1986a. *Latinos in the United States: The sacred and the political.* Notre Dame, IN: Notre Dame Press.

_____. 1986b. Latinos and the sacred. *Cross Currents* (Fall): 300-322.

_____. 1992. Rediscovering the sacred. *Latino Studies Journal* 3, no. 2 (May): 1-25.

_____. 1993. *The Latino family and the politics of transformation.* London and Westport, CT: Praeger Press.

_____. 1994. "The personal, historical and sacred grounding of culture: Some reflections on the creation of Latino culture in the U.S. from the perspective of the Theory of Transformation." In *Old masks, new faces: Religion and Latino identities,* edited by Anthony M. Stevens-Arroyo and Gilbert R. Cadena, 143-172. Vol. 2 of PARAL Studies Series. New York: Bildner Center Books.

Acosta, Oscar Zeta. 1989. [Chapter 1]. In *The revolt of the cockroach people,* 11-21. New York: Vintage Books.

Alarcón, Norma. 1989. Traddutora, traditora: A paradigmatic figure of Chicana feminism. *Cultural Critique* (Fall): 57-87.

Alegría, Ricardo. 1954. *La Fiesta de Santiago Apóstol en Loaiza Aldea.* San Juan, PR: Estudios Puertorriqueños.

Alegría, Ricardo E. 1983. *La vida de Jesucristo según el santero puertorriqueño Florencio Cabán.* San Juan, PR: Centro de Estudios Avanzados de Puerto Rico y el Caribe.

Almaraz, Félix D., Jr. 1989. *The San Antonio missions and their system of land tenure.* Austin, TX: University of Texas Press.

Amaro, Hortensia. 1988. Considerations for prevention of HIV infection among Hispanic women. *Psychology of Women Quarterly* 12 (December): 429-443.

Anaya, Rudolfo A., and Francisco A. Lomeli, eds. 1989. *Aztlan: Essays on the Chicano homeland.* Albuquerque, NM: Academia/El Norte Publications.

Bach-y-Rita, George. 1982. "The Mexican-American: Religious and cultural influences." In *Mental health and Hispanic Americans: Clinical perspectives,* edited by Rosina M. Becerra, Marvin Karno, and Javier I. Escobar, 29-40. New York: Grune & Stratton.

Badillo, David. 1994. "The Catholic Church and the making of Mexican-American parish communities in the Midwest." In *Mexican Americans and the Catholic Church, 1900-1965,* edited by Jay P. Dolan and Gilberto M. Hinojosa, 237-308. Notre Dame, IN: University of Notre Dame Press.

Banker, Mark T. 1987. "Missionary to his own people: José Ynes Perea and Hispanic Presbyterianism in New Mexico." In *Religion and society in the American West: Historical essays,* edited by Carl Guarneri and David Alvarez, 79-104. Lanham, MD: University Press of America.

Bascom, William R. 1969. *Ifà divination: Communication between gods and men in West Africa.* Bloomington, IN: Indiana University Press.

Beirne, Charles J. 1975. *The Problem of Americanization in the Catholic Schools of Puerto Rico.* Río Piedras, PR: Editorial Universitaria.

Benavides, Gustavo. 1994a. "Resistance and accommodation in Latin American popular religiosity." In *An enduring flame: Studies on Latino popular religiosity,* edited by Anthony M. Stevens-Arroyo and Ana María Díaz-Stevens, 37-68. Vol. 1 of PARAL Studies Series. New York: Bildner Center Books.

_____. 1994b. "Syncretism and legitimacy in Latin American religion." In *Enigmatic powers: Syncretism with African and Indigenous peoples' religions among Latinos,* edited by Anthony M. Stevens-Arroyo and Andrés I. Pérez y Mena, 19-46. Vol. 3 of PARAL Studies Series. New York: Bildner Center Books.

Bennett, Spencer. 1989. "Civil religion in a new context." In *Religion and political power,* edited by G. Benavides and M. Daly, 151-166. Albany: State University of New York Press.

Berardi, Gayle K. 1989. The role of church amnesty assistance programs in the implementation of the 1986 Immigration Reform and Control Act. *Journal of Borderland Studies* 4, no. 2 (Fall):59-69.

Bosniak, Lindie. 1984. Crackdown on sanctuary: The underground railroad surfaces. *NACLA* 18, no.3 (May-June):4-7.

Brackenridge, Douglas. 1974. *Iglesia presbiteriana: A history of Presbyterians and Mexican Americans in the Southwest.* San Antonio: Trinity University Press.

Burns, Jeffrey M. 1987a. "The Mexican-American Catholic Community in California, 1850-1980." In *Religion and society in the American West: Historical essays,* edited by Carl Guarneri and David Alvarez, 255-273. Lanham, MD: University Press of America.

_____. 1987b. "The Mexican-American Catholic Community." In *The American Catholic Parish: A history from 1850 to the present,* Vol. 2, edited by Jay P. Dolan, 79-86. New York: Paulist Press.

_____. 1994. "The Mexican Catholic community in California." In *Mexican Americans and the Catholic Church, 1900-1965,* edited by Jay P. Dolan and Gilberto M. Hinojosa, 129-236. Notre Dame, IN: University of Notre Dame Press.

Cadena, Gilbert R. 1989. Chicano clergy and the emergence of Liberation Theology. *Hispanic Journal of Behavioral Sciences* 11, no. 2 (May): 107-121.

_____. 1994. "Religious ethnic identity: A socio-religious portrait of Latinos and Latinas in the Catholic church." In *Old masks, new faces: Religion and Latino identities,* edited by Anthony M. Stevens-Arroyo and Gilbert R. Cadena, 33-59. Vol. 2 of PARAL Studies Series. New York: Bildner Center Books.

_____. Forthcoming. *Catholicism and Chicano empowerment: Cultural resistance and Liberation Theology.* Austin, TX: University of Texas Press.

Campa, Arthur Leon. n.d. *Spanish religious folktheatre in the Southwest: Second cycle.* Albuquerque, NM: University of New Mexico Press.

Campbell, Frances M. 1987. "Missiology in New Mexico, 1850-1900: The success and failure of Catholic education." In *Religion and society in the American West: Historical essays,* edited by Carl Guarneri and David Alvarez, 59-77. Lanham, MD: University Press of America.

Canino Salgado, Marcelino. 1974. *Gozos devocionales de la tradición puertorriqueña*. Río Piedras, PR: Editorial Universitaria.

Carrasco, David. 1982a. *Quetzalcoatl and the irony of empire: Myths and prophesies in the Aztec tradition*. Chicago: University of Chicago Press.

_____. 1982b. A perspective for a study of religious dimensions in Chicano experiences: *Bless me, Ultima* as a religious text. *Aztlan* 13, no. 1, 2 (Spring/Fall): 195-222.

_____. 1990. "The religion of the Aztecs: Ways of the warrior, words of the sage." In *Religions of Mesoamerica: Cosmovision and ceremonial centers*, 58-91. San Francisco: Harper and Row.

_____. 1991. "The sacrifice of Tezcatlipoca: To change place." In *To change place: Aztec ceremonial landscapes*, 31-57. Boulder: University of Colorado Press.

_____. 1992. "Myth, cosmic terror, and the Templo Mayor." In *The Great Temple of Tenochtitlán: Center and periphery in the Aztec world*, edited by Johanna Broda, David Carrasco, and Eduardo Matos Moctezuma, 186-236. Berkeley: University of California Press.

_____. 1994. "Jaguar Christians in the contact zone." In *Enigmatic powers: Syncretism with African and Indigenous peoples' religions among Latinos*, edited by Anthony M. Stevens-Arroyo and Andrés I. Pérez y Mena, 69-79. Vol. 3 of PARAL Studies Series. New York: Bildner Center Books.

Carrillo, Alberto. 1971. The sociological failures of the Catholic Church towards the Chicano. *The Journal of Mexican American Studies* 1, no. 2 (Winter): 75-83.

Casey, Genevieve M. 1989. "El Padre Kern." In *Father Clem Kern: Conscience of Detroit*, 118-158. Detroit, MI: Marygrove College, in cooperation with the Fr. Clement H. Kern Foundation.

Castañeda, Carlos E. 1974. *Church views of the Mexican American*. New York: Arno Press.

Castellanos, Isabel. 1990. Grammatical structure, historical development, and religious usage of Afro-Cuban Bozal speech. *Folklore Forum* 23, no. 1, 2: 57-84.

_____. 1992. "Notes on Afro-Cuban religion and Cuban linguistics." In *Cuban studies since the revolution*, edited by Damián Fernández. Gainesville, FL: University Press of Florida.

Castillo, Ana. 1993. "An interlude: On Francisco el Penitente's first becoming a santero and thereby sealing his fate." In *So far from God*, 94-102. New York: Norton.

Chalfant, H. Paul, Peter L. Heller, et al. 1990. The clergy as a resource for those encountering psychological distress. *Review of Religious Research* 31 (March): 305-313.

Codega, Susan A., Kay B. Pasley, and Jill Kreutzer. 1990. Coping behaviors of adolescent mothers: An exploratory study and comparison of Mexican-Americans and Anglos. *Journal of Adolescent Research* 5 (January): 34-53.

Comas-Díaz, Lillian. 1989. "Culturally relevant issues and treatment implications for Hispanics." In *Crossing cultures in mental health*, edited by Diane R. Koslown and Elizabeth Pathy Salett, 31-48. Washington, DC: SIETAR International.

Cook, Scott. 1965. The Prophets: A revivalistic folk religious movement in Puerto Rico. *Caribbean Studies* 4 (January): 20-35. Reprinted, 1971, in *Peoples and Cultures of the Caribbean*, edited by Michael M. Horowitz, 560-579. Garden City: The Natural History Press.

Cooper Alarcón, Daniel. 1992. The Aztec palimpsest: Toward a new understanding of Aztlán, cultural identity and history. *Aztlán: Journal of Chicano Studies* 19, no. 2: 33-68.

Cortés, Carlos E., ed. 1980. *Protestantism and Latinos in the United States*. New York: Arno Press.

Crocker, Ruth Hutchinson. 1987. "Gary Mexicans and Christian Americanization: A study in cultural conflict." In *Forging a community: The Latino experience in northwest Indiana, 1919-1975*, edited by James B. Lane and Edward J. Escobar, 115-134. Calumet, IL: Calumet Regional Archives and Cattails Press.

Cruz, David. 1977. Raised eyebrows and no crucifixes. *Nuestro* 1, no. 7 (October).

Curbelo de Díaz González, Irene. 1970. *Santos de Puerto Rico*. San Juan: Museo de Santos.

Curtis, James. 1980. Miami's Little Havana yard shrines: Cult, religion, and landscape. *Journal of Cultural Geography* 1, 1: 1-15.

Cutter, Donald C. 1984. With a little help from their saints. *Pacific Historical Review* 53, no. 2: 123-140.

Davis, Kenneth. 1994a. "Brevia from the Hispanic shift: Continuity rather than conversion?" In *An enduring flame: Studies on Latino popular religiosity*, edited by Anthony M. Stevens-Arroyo and Ana

María Díaz-Stevens, 205-210. Vol. 1 of PARAL Studies Series. New York: Bildner Center Books.

_____. 1994b. *Primero Dios.* Susquehanna, PA: Susquehanna University Press.

Daydi-Tolson, Santiago. 1988. "Ritual and religion in Tomás Rivera's work." In *Tomás Rivera 1935-1984: The man and his work,* edited by Vernon E. Lattin, et al, 136-149. Tempe, AZ: Bilingual Review Press.

De Aragón, Ray John. 1978. *Padre Martínez and Bishop Lamy.* Las Vegas, NM: Pan American Publishing Co.

Díaz Ramírez, Ana María. 1980. "The life, passion, and death of the Spanish-speaking apostolate of the Archdiocese of New York." In *Prophets denied honor,* edited by Antonio M. Stevens-Arroyo, 208-213. Maryknoll, NY: Orbis Books.

Díaz-Stevens, Ana María. 1974. Christmas comes from the mountains: A celebration of Christmas in Puerto Rico. *Response* (December):22-25.

_____. 1975. Religion in the melting pot of the Caribbean: San Juan, Puerto Rico. *New World Outlook* (May): 8-15. Reprinted, 1980, in *Prophets denied honor,* edited by Antonio M. Stevens-Arroyo, 336-338. Maryknoll, NY: Orbis Books.

_____. 1977. A flock that is being left untended. *Nuestro* (October): 60.

_____. 1987a. A concept of mission: The national parish and Francis Cardinal Spellman. *Migration World* 15, no. 1: 22- 26.

_____. 1987b. An archdiocese in ferment: No longer the powerhouse. Interview in *New York Newsday* (September 17): sec. 2, 3,11.

_____. 1990. From Puerto Rican to Hispanic: The politics of the fiestas patronales in New York. *Latino Studies Journal* 1, no. 1 (January): 28-47.

_____. 1991a. Church's challenge: Serving needs of burgeoning Latino ranks. Interview by Paul Moses, *New York Newsday* (October 14): 6, 23-24.

_____. 1991b. Social distance and religious conflict in the pre-Vatican Catholicism of Puerto Rico. *MACLAS Essays* (Journal of the Middle Atlantic Council for Latin American Studies) 4: 291-299.

_____. 1993a. *Oxcart Catholicism on Fifth Avenue.* Notre Dame, IN: University of Notre Dame Press.

_____. 1993b. La Misa Jíbara como campo de batalla ideológica. *Revista de Ciencias Sociales* (Universidad de Puerto Rico) 30, no. 1-2 (January-June): 139-161.

_____. 1993c. The saving grace: The matriarchal core of Latino Catholicism. *Latino Studies Journal* 4, no. 3 (September): 60-78.

_____. 1994a. "Analyzing popular religiosity for socio-religious meaning." In *An enduring flame: Studies on Latino popular religiosity,* edited by Anthony M. Stevens-Arroyo and Ana María Díaz-Stevens, 17-36. Vol. 1 of PARAL Studies Series. New York: Bildner Center Books.

_____. 1994b. Ministerio y cambio social. *Cristianismo y Sociedad* [Guayaquil, Ecuador] 31-32, no. 118-119: 29-42.

_____. 1994c. "Latinas and the church." In *Hispanic Catholic culture in the U.S.: Issues and concerns,* edited by Jay P. Dolan and Allan Figueroa Deck, 240-277. Notre Dame, IN: University of Notre Dame Press.

_____. 1994d. "Latino youth and the church." In *Hispanic Catholic culture in the U.S.: Issues and concerns,* edited by Jay P. Dolan and Allan Figueroa Deck, 278-307. Notre Dame, IN: University of Notre Dame Press.

Díaz-Stevens, Ana María, and Antonio M. Stevens-Arroyo. 1982. "Puerto Ricans in the States." In *The minority report,* edited by A. G. Dworkin and R. J. Dworkin, 196-232. 2d ed. New York: Holt, Rinehart & Winston.

_____. 1994. "Religion and faith among Latinos." In *Handbook of Hispanic cultures in the United States,* edited by Félix Padilla. Houston, TX: Arte Público Press.

Diekemper, Barnabas C. 1985. The Catholic Church in the shadows: The southwestern United States during the Mexican period. *Journal of the West* 24, no. 2: 46-53.

Do Campo, Orlando. 1994. "The Supreme Court and the practice of Santería." In *Enigmatic powers: Syncretism with African and Indigenous peoples' religions among Latinos,* edited by Anthony M. Stevens-Arroyo and Andrés I. Pérez y Mena, 159- 179. Vol. 3 of PARAL Studies Series. New York: Bildner Center Books.

Dolan, Jay P. 1987. The new religious history. *Reviews in American History* 15 (September): 449-454.

_____. 1989. "Religion and Social Change in the American Catholic Community." In *Altered landscapes: Christianity in America,* edited by D. Lotz, 42-60. Grand Rapids, MI: Eerdmans.

_____. 1992. *The American Catholic experience: A history from colonial times to the present.* Notre Dame, IN: Notre Dame Press.

Dolan, Jay P., and Gilberto M. Hinojosa, eds. 1994. *Mexican Americans and the Catholic Church, 1900-1965.* Notre Dame and London: University of Notre Dame Press.

Dolan, Jay P., and Jaime Vidal, eds. 1994. *Puerto Rican and Cuban Catholics in the U.S., 1900-1965.* Notre Dame and London: University of Notre Dame Press.

Dolan, Jay P., and Allan Figueroa Deck, S.J., eds. 1994. *Hispanic Catholic culture in the U.S.: Issues and concerns.* Notre Dame and London: University of Notre Dame Press.

Domino, George. 1981. Attitudes toward suicide among Mexican American and Anglo youth. *Hispanic Journal of Behavioral Sciences* 3, no. 4 (December): 385-395.

Dressler, William W. 1985. Stress and sorcery in three social groups. *International Journal of Social Psychiatry* 31 (Winter): 275-281.

Eighme Ahlborn, Richard. 1986. *The Penitente moradas of Abiquiú.* Washington: Smithsonian Institute.

Elford, George. 1983. Catholic schools and bilingual education. *Momentum* 14, no. 1 (February): 35-37.

Elizondo, Virgilio. 1974. *Anthropological and psychological characteristics of the Mexican American.* San Antonio, TX: Mexican American Cultural Center.

_____. 1980. "The Mexican American as seen from within." In *Prophets denied honor,* edited by Anthony M. Stevens-Arroyo, 5-7. Maryknoll, NY: Orbis Books.

_____. 1994. "Popular religion as the core of cultural identity in the Mexican American experience." In *An enduring flame: Studies on Latino popular religiosity,* edited by Anthony M. Stevens-Arroyo and Ana María Díaz-Stevens, 113-132. Vol. 1 of PARAL Studies Series. New York: Bildner Center Books.

Escabí, Pedro, and Elsa Escabí. 1976. *La Décima: Estudios etnográficos de la cultura popular de Puerto Rico.* Río Piedras, PR: Editorial Universitaria.

Escobar, Edward J. 1987. "The forging of a community." In *Forging a community: The Latino experience in northwest Indiana, 1919-1975,* edited by James B. Lane and Edward J. Escobar, 3-24. Calumet, IL: Calumet Regional Archives and Cattails Press.

Espinoza, Manuel J. 1993. The origin of the Penitentes of New Mexico: Separating fact from fiction. *The Catholic Historical Review* 79, no. 3 (July): 454-477.

Estévez, Felipe J. 1983. The Hispanic search beyond biculturalism. *Theological Education* 20 (Autumn): 58-64.

_____. 1989a. *El perfil pastoral de Félix Varela*. Miami: Editorial Universal.

_____. 1989b. *Félix Varela, letters to Elpidio: A critical translation*. New York: Paulist Press.

Fayer, Joan M., Alma Simounet de Geigel, and Joseph M. Ferri. 1985. Puerto Rican identity: Themes that unite and divide. *Journal of American Culture* 8 (Winter): 83-91.

Figueroa Deck, Allan. 1979. A new vision of a tattered friendship. *Grito del Sol* 4, no. 1: 87-93.

_____. 1983. "The worldview, values and religion of Mexican immigrants in Orange today." In *Second lives,* 71-73. Santa Ana, CA: South Coast Repertory Publications.

_____. 1985. Fundamentalism and the Hispanic Catholic. *America* 152, no. 3 (January 26): 64-66.

_____. 1987. Multicultural sensitivities. *Human Development* 8, no. 2 (Summer): 32-34.

_____. 1988. Proselytism and Hispanic Catholics: How long can we cry wolf? *America* 159, no. 18 (December 10): 485-490.

_____. 1990. The crisis of Hispanic ministry: Multiculturalism as an ideology. *America* 163, no. 2 (July 14-21): 33-36.

Figueroa Deck, Allan, and José Armando Nuñez. 1982. Religious enthusiasm and Hispanic youth. *America* (October 23): 232- 234.

Fitzpatrick, Joseph P., SJ. 1971. *Puerto Rican Americans: The meaning of migration to the mainland*. Englewood Cliffs, NJ: Prentice Hall.

_____. 1983. "Faith and stability among Hispanic families: The role of religion in cultural transition." In *Families and religions,* edited by W. D'Antonio and J. Aldous, 221-242. Beverly Hills: Sage Publications.

_____. 1989. Puerto Ricans as a social minority on the mainland. *International Journal of Group Tensions* 19 (Fall): 195-208.

_____. 1990. Catholic responses to Hispanic newcomers. *Sociological Focus* 23 (August): 155-166.

_____. 1994. "The dilemma of social research and social policy: The Puerto Rican case, 1953-1993." In *Old masks, new faces:*

Religion and Latino identities, edited by Anthony M. Stevens-Arroyo and Gilbert R. Cadena, 173-181. Vol. 2 of PARAL Studies Series. New York: Bildner Center Books.

Fitzpatrick, Joseph P., SJ., and Douglas Gurak. 1982. Intermarriage among Hispanic ethnic groups in New York City. *American Journal of Sociology* 87, no. 4 (January): 921-934.

Flores, Richard R. 1994. "Para el Niño Dios: Sociability and commemorative sentiment in popular religious practice." In *An enduring flame: Studies on Latino popular religiosity,* edited by Anthony M. Stevens-Arroyo and Ana María Díaz- Stevens, 171-190. Vol. 1 of PARAL Studies Series. New York: Bildner Center Books.

Flores, Robert, Silvia Novo-Peña, and Guillermo Pulido. 1982. *Interiores: Aspectos seculares de la religión/ Interiors: Secular aspects of religion.* Houston, TX: D.H. White Co.

Forste, Renata T., and Tim B. Heaton. 1988. Initiation of sexual activity among female adolescents. *Youth and Society* 19, no. 3 (March): 250-268.

Fox, Steve. 1994. Sacred pedestrians: The many faces of Southwest pilgrimage. *Journal of the Southwest* 1 (Spring): 33-53.

Gallup Organization. 1978. *A study of religious and social attitudes of Hispanic Americans.* Princeton, NJ: The Gallup Organization Inc.

Gamba, Raymond J., and Gerardo Marín. 1993. The role of expectations in religious conversions: The case of Hispanic Catholics. *Review of Religious Research* 34 (June): 357-371.

Gabriel, Rosemary, ed. 1992. *Santos de Palo: The household saints of Puerto Rico.* New York: Museum of American Folk Art.

Gannon, M.V. 1983. *The cross in the sand: The early Catholic Church in Florida, 1513-1870,* 2d. ed. Gainesville, FL: University Presses of Florida.

García, F. Chris, and Thomas A. Rehfeld. 1987. *A survey investigating the socio-political opinions of Hispanics and Non-Hispanics in the Southwest and the perceived influence of the Catholic Church.* Albuquerque, NM: Zia Research Associates.

García, Juan R., and Angela Cal. 1987. "El Círculo de Obreros Católicos 'San José', 1925 to 1930." In *Forging a community: The Latino experience in northwest Indiana, 1919-1975,* edited by James B. Lane and Edward J. Escobar, 95-114. Calumet, IL: Calumet Regional Archives and Cattails Press.

Garrido, Pablo. 1952. *Esotería y fervor populares de Puerto Rico.* Madrid: Ediciones Cultura Hispánica.

Garrison, Vivian. 1974. "Sectarianism and psychological adjustment: A controlled comparison of Puerto Rican Pentecostals and Catholics." In *Religious Movements in Contemporary America,* edited by I. Zaretsky, 298-329. Princeton, NJ: Princeton University Press.

_____. 1977. "The Puerto Rican syndrome in psychiatry and Espiritismo." In *Case Studies in Spirit Possession,* edited by Vincent Crapanzano and Vivian Garrison, 383-449. New York: John Wiley and Sons.

Garzón, Fernando, and Tan Siang-Yang. 1992. Counseling Hispanics: Cross-cultural and Christian perspectives. *Journal of Psychology and Christianity* 11 (Winter): 378-390.

Gibson, John W., and Jean B. Lanz. 1991. Factors associated with Hispanic teenagers' attitude toward the importance of birth control. *Child and Adolescent Social Work Journal* 8, no. 5 (October): 399-415.

Goldsmith, Raquel Rubio. 1987. "Shipwrecked in the desert: A short history of the Mexican Sisters of the House of the Providence in Douglas, Arizona, 1927-1949." In *Women on the U.S.-Mexico border: Responses to change,* edited by Vicky L. Ruiz and Susan Tiano, 177-195. Boston, MA: Allen and Unwin.

Gómez, David. 1973. *Somos Chicanos: Strangers in our own land.* Boston, MA: Beacon Press.

_____. 1980. "El movimiento Chicano." Excerpted in *Prophets denied honor,* eidted by Antonio M. Stevens-Arroyo, 5-7. Maryknoll, NY: Orbis Books.

González, Deena J. 1992. "Encountering Columbus." In *Chicano studies: Critical connections between research and community,* 13-19. The National Association for Chicano Studies.

González, Juan. 1983. Caribbean Voodoo: A Catholic response, a private encounter. *Nuestro* 7, no. 1 (January-February): 37.

González, Roberto O., and Michael LaVelle. 1985. *The Hispanic Catholic in the United States: A socio-cultural and religious profile.* Vol. 1 of Hispanic American Pastoral Investigations. New York: Northeast Catholic Pastoral Center.

González, William. 1981. "The religious ballad of New Mexico and the Canary Islands: A comparative study of traditional features." In *Oral traditional literature: A Festschrift for Albert Bates Lord,* edited by John Miles Foley, 294-300. Columbus, OH: Slavica.

González-Wippler, Migene. 1982. *The Santería experience.* Englewood Cliffs, NJ: Prentice Hall.

_____. 1989. *Santería: The religion: A legacy of faith, rites, and magic.* New York: Harmony Books.

_____. 1994. "Santería: Its dynamics and multiple roots." In *Enigmatic powers: Syncretism with African and Indigenous peoples' religions among Latinos,* edited by Anthony M. Stevens-Arroyo and Andrés I. Pérez y Mena, 99-111 . Vol. 3 of PARAL Studies Series. New York: Bildner Center Books.

Goris, Anneris. 1994. "Rites for a rising nationalism: Religious meaning and Dominican community identity in New York City." In *Old masks, new faces: Religion and Latino identities,* edited by Anthony M. Stevens-Arroyo and Gilbert R. Cadena, 117-141. Vol. 2 of PARAL Studies Series. New York: Bildner Center Books.

Graham, Joe S. 1976. "The role of the curandero in the Mexican American folk medicine system in west Texas." In *American folk medicine,* edited by Wayland D. Hand, 175-189. Berkeley, CA: University of California Press.

Greeley, Andrew. 1988. Defection among Hispanics. *America* 159, no. 3 (July 23-30): 61-62.

Gregory, Steven. 1987. "Afro-Caribbean religions in New York City: The case of Santería." In *Caribbean life in New York City: Sociocultural dimensions,* edited by Constance R. Sutton and Elsa M. Chaney, 287-302. New York: Center for Migration Studies.

Griswold del Castillo, Richard. 1984. *La familia: Chicano families in the urban Southwest, 1848 to the present.* Notre Dame, IN: University of Notre Dame Press.

Hardwood, Alan. 1971. "The hot-cold theory of disease: Implications for treatment of Puerto Rican patients." *Journal of the American Medical Association* 216, no. 7: 1153-58.

_____. 1977a. Puerto Rican Spiritism. Parts 1-2. *Culture, Medicine and Psychiatry* 1 no. 1 (April): 69-95; 1, no. 2: 135-153.

_____. 1977b. RX: Spiritist as needed; A study of a Puerto Rican community mental health resource. New York: John Wiley and Sons.

Hayes-Bautista, David E. 1992. Academe can take the lead in binding together the residents of a multicultural society. *The Chronicle of Higher Education* (October 28): B, 1-2.

Hayes-Bautista, David E., and Jorge Chapa. 1988. Latino terminology: Conceptual bases for standardized terminology. *American Journal of Public Health* 77: 61-68.

Hayes-Bautista, David E., Aída Hurtado, R. Burciaga Valdez, and Anthony C.R. Hernández. 1992. *No longer a minority: Latinos and social policy in California*. Los Angeles: UCLA, Chicano Studies Research Center.

Hennelly, Alfred T. 1983. "Grassroots communities: A new model of church?" In *Tracing the spirit,* edited by J. Hug, 60-82. New York: Paulist Press.

Hernández, Edwin. 1994. "Relocating the sacred among Latinos: Reflections on methodology." In *Old masks, new faces: Religion and Latino identities,* edited by Anthony M. Stevens-Arroyo and Gilbert R. Cadena, 61-76. Vol. 2 of PARAL Studies Series. New York: Bildner Center Books.

Hernández, Edwin I., and Roger L. Dudley. 1990. Persistence of religion through primary group ties among Hispanic Seventh- Day Adventist young people. *Review of Religious Research* 32 (December): 157-172.

Hinojosa, Gilberto M. 1994. "Mexican-American faith communities in Texas and the Southwest." In *Mexican Americans and the Catholic Church, 1900-1965,* edited by Jay P. Dolan and Gilberto M. Hinojosa, 11-128. Notre Dame, IN: University of Notre Dame Press.

Horowitz, Ruth. 1983. *Honor and the American dream: Culture and identity in a Chicano community.* New Brunswick: Rutgers University Press.

Hough, Richard L. 1982. "Religion and pluralism among the Spanish-speaking groups of the Southwest." In *Politics and society in the Southwest: Ethinicity and Chicano pluralism,* edited by Z. Anthony Kruszewski, Richard L. Hough, and Jacob Ornstein Galicia, 169 195. Boulder, CO: Westview Press.

Hughes, Cornelius. 1992. Views from the pews: Hispanic and Anglo Catholics in a changing church. *Review of Religious Research* 33, no. 4 (June): 364-375.

Hurtado, Aída, David E. Hayes-Bautista, R. Burciaga Valdez, and Anthony C.R. Hernández. 1992. *Redefining California: Latino social engagement in a multicultural society.* Los Angeles: UCLA, Chicano Studies Research Center.

Hurtado, Juan. 1976. *An attitudinal study of social distance between the Mexican American and the church.* San Antonio, TX: Mexican American Cultural Center.

_____. 1979. The social interaction between the Chicano and the church: An historical perspective. *Grito del Sol* 4, no. 1: 25-45.

Hutchison, Ray. 1988. The Hispanic community in Chicago: A study of population growth and acculturation. *Research in Race and Ethnic Relations* 5: 193-229.

Idowu, B.E. 1961. *Olodumare: God in Yoruba belief.* London: Longmans Green and Co.

Isais, A. Raoul. 1979. The Chicano and the American Catholic Church. *Grito del Sol* 4, no. 1 (Winter): 9-24.

Isasi-Díaz, Ada María. 1994. "The cultural identity of the Latino woman: The cross-disciplinary perspective of Mujerista theology." In *Old masks, new faces: Religion and Latino identities,* edited by Anthony M. Stevens-Arroyo and Gilbert R. Cadena, 93-116. Vol. 2 of PARAL Studies Series. New York: Bildner Center Books.

Jensen, Carol L. 1987. "Religion and Ethnicity." In *The American Catholic parish: A history from 1850 to the present,* Vol. 2, edited by Jay P. Dolan, 199-228. New York: Paulist Press.

Jiménez, Ricardo. 1983. Understanding the culture and learning styles of Hispanic students. *Momentum* 14, no. 1 (February): 15-18.

Juárez, José Roberto. 1974. La iglesia católica y el chicano en sud Texas, 1836-1911. *Aztlán* 4, no. 2 (Fall): 217-255.

Kay, Margarita Artschwager. 1977. "Health and illness in a Mexican American barrio." In *Ethnic medicine in the Southwest,* edited by E. Spicer, 99-166. Tucson AZ: University of Arizona Press.

Keefe, Susan E., and Amado M. Padilla. 1987. *Chicano ethnicity.* Albuquerque, NM: University of New Mexico Press.

Kenney, Bradford, Ronald Cromwell, and Edwin Vaughn. 1977. Identifying the socio-contextual forms of religiosity among ethnic minority group members. *Journal for the Scientific Study of Religion* 16, no. 3: 237-244.

Koss, Joan D. 1972. The why of religious cults: The case of Spiritualism in Puerto Rico. *Revista de Ciencias Sociales* 16, no. 1 (March): 61-72.

_____. 1975. Therapeutic aspects of Puerto Rican cult practices. *Psychiatry* 38, no. 2 (May): 160-171.

_____. 1977. "Spirits as socializing agents: A case study of a Puerto Rican girl reared in a matricentric family." In *Case Studies in Spirit Possession,* edited by Vincent Crapanzano and Vivian Garrison, 365-382. New York: John Wiley and Sons.

Koss-Chioino, Joan. 1992. *Women as healers: Women as patients, mental health care and traditional healing in Puerto Rico.* Boulder, CO: Westview Press.

Lachaga, José Mª de. 1982. *El pueblo hispano en USA: Minorías étnicas y la iglesia católica.* Bilbao, Spain: Desclée de Brouwer.

Lafaye, Jacques. 1974. *Quetzacoatl and Guadalupe: The formation of Mexican national consciousness: 1531-1813.* Chicago: University of Chicago Press.

Lampe, Philip E. 1975. Acculturation of Mexican Americans in public and parochial schools. *Sociological Analysis: A Journal in the Sociology of Religion* 36 (Spring): 57-66.

_____. 1976. Assimilation and the school system. *Sociological Analysis: A Journal in the Sociology of Religion* 37 (Fall): 228-242.

_____. 1977. Religion and the assimilation of Mexican Americans. *Review of Religious Research* 18, no. 3 (Spring): 243-253.

_____. 1986. Our Lady of Guadalupe and ethnic prejudice. *Borderlands Journal* 9, no. 1 (Spring): 91-120.

_____. 1993. *Hispanics in the Church: Up from the cellar.* San Francisco: Catholic Scholars Press.

Larson, Vicki. 1990. The flight of the faithful. *Hispanic* (November): 18-24.

LaRuffa, Anthony L. 1969. Cultural change and Pentecostalism in Puerto Rico. *Social and Economic Studies* 18 (September): 273-81.

_____. 1971. *San Cipriano: Life in a Puerto Rican Community.* New York: Gordon and Breach.

Lauria, Anthony, Jr. 1964. Respeto, relajo and interpersonal relations in Puerto Rico. *Anthropological Quarterly* 37: 53-67. Reprinted, 1968, in *Puerto Rican children in mainland schools,* edited by Francesco Cordasco and Eugene Bucchioni, 42-54. Metuchen, NJ: Scarecrow Press.

Leatham, Miguel. 1989. Indigenista hermeneutics and the historical meaning of Our Lady of Guadalupe of Mexico. *Folklore Forum* 22: 27-40.

Lennon, John J. 1976. *A comparative study of the patterns of acculturation of selected Puerto Rican Protestant and Roman Catholic families in an urban metropolitan area.* Chicago: R and E Research Associates.

León, Luis D.G. 1994. Somos un cuerpo en Cristo: Notes on power and the body in an East Los Angeles Chicano/Mexicano Pentecostal community. *Latino Studies Journal* 5, no. 3 (September): 60-86.

León-Portillo, Miguel, ed. 1990. *The broken spears: The Aztec account of the conquest of Mexico.* Boston: Beacon Press.

Levin, Jeffrey S., and Kyriakos S. Markides. 1985. Religion and health in Mexican Americans. *Journal of Religion and Health* 24 (Spring): 60-69.

_____. 1986. Religious attendance and subjective health. *Journal for the Scientific Study of Religion* 25, no. 1 (March): 31- 40.

_____. 1988. Religious attendance and psychological well-being in middle-aged and older Mexican Americans. *Sociological Analysis: A Journal in the Sociology of Religion* 49 (Spring): 66-72.

_____. 1991. Religious involvement among Hispanic and Black mothers of newborns. *Hispanic Journal of Behavioral Sciences* 13, no. 4 (November): 436-447.

López Cruz, Francisco. 1967. *La música folklórica de Puerto Rico.* Sharon, CT: Troutman Press.

Macheboeuf, Joseph P., and Jean Baptiste Lamy. 1971. "The work of Archbishop Lamy in New Mexico." In *A documentary history of Mexican Americans,* edited by Wayne Moquin, 285-295. New York: Praeger.

Macklin, June. 1975. "Belief, ritual and healing: New England spiritualism and Mexican-American spiritism compared." In *Religious movements in contemporary America,* edited by Irving I. Zaretsky and Mark P. Leone, 383-417. Princeton, NJ: Princeton University Press.

Macklin, June, and Alvina Teniente de Costilla. 1979a. "La Virgen de Guadalupe and the American dream: The melting pot bubbles in Toledo, Ohio." In *The Chicano experience,* edited by Stanley West and June Macklin. Boulder, CO: Westview Press.

_____. 1979b. "Curanderismo and Espiritismo: Complementary approaches to traditional mental health services." In *The Chicano experience,* edited by Stanley West and June Macklin, 207-226. Boulder, CO: Westview.

Maduro, Otto. 1994. "Directions for a reassessment of Latino/a religion." In *Enigmatic powers: Syncretism with African and Indigenous peoples' religions among Latinos,* edited by Anthony M. Stevens-Arroyo and Andrés I. Pérez y Mena, 47-68. Vol.3 of PARAL Studies Series. New York: Bildner Center Books.

Maduro, Otto, ed. 1994. *Cristianismo y Sociedad* [Special issue on Religion among Latinos in the U.S.A] 31-32, no. 118-119 (January-March) [Guayaquil, Ecuador].

Mailer, Norman. 1974. *The faith of graffiti.* New York: Praeger.

Maldonado-Denis, Manuel. 1980. *The emigration dialectic: Puerto Rico and the U.S.A.* New York: International Publishers.

Maldonado, James S. 1974. Father Benedict Cuesta: A priest and his work. *La Luz* 3, no. 5 (August): 15-18.

Mares, E.A. 1983. "Hispanic humanities resources of New Mexico." In *Hispanics and the humanities in the Southwest: A directory of resources,* edited by F. Arturo Rosales and David William Foster, 175-186. Tempe, AZ: Center for Latin American Studies, Arizona State University.

Markides, Kyriakos S. 1983. Aging, religiosity, and adjustment: Alongitudinal analysis. *Journal of Gerontology* 38, no. 5 (September):621 625.

Markides, Kyriakos S., and Thomas, Cole. 1984. Change and continuity in Mexican American religious behavior: A three- generation study. *Social Science Quarterly* 65, no. 2 (June): 618-625.

Markides, Kyriakos S., et al. 1987. Religion, aging, and life satisfaction: An eight-year, three-wave longitudinal study. *Gerontologist* 27, no. 5 (October): 660-665.

Marqués, René. 1976. *The docile Puerto Rican.* Translated by Barbara Bockus Aponte (1963). Philadelphia, PA: Temple University Press.

Martínez, Cervando, Jr. 1988. "Mexican-Americans." In *Clinical guidelines in cross-cultural mental health,* edited by Lillian Comas Díaz and Ezra E.H. Griffith, 182-203. New York: John Wiley & Sons.

McCready, William. 1985. "Culture and religion." In *Hispanics in the United States,* edited by Pastora San Juan Cafferty and William C. McCready. New Brunswick, NJ: Transaction Books.

McGuire, Meredith. 1994a. "Linking theory and methodology for the study of Latino religiosity in the United States context." In *An enduring flame: Studies on Latino popular religiosity,* edited by Anthony M. Stevens-Arroyo and Ana María Díaz-Stevens, 191-

204. Vol. 1 of PARAL Studies Series New York: Bildner Center Books.

_____. 1994b. Religiosidad sí; marginalidad no: Porque la sociología de la religión no puede darse el lujo de marginar la religión latina. *Cristianismo y Sociedad [Guayaquil, Ecuador]* 31-32, no. 118-19: 9-18.

McMurtrey, Martin. 1987. *Mariachi Bishop: The life story of Patrick Flores.* San Antonio, TX: Corona Publishing Co.

McNally, Michael J. 1984. *Catholicism in south Florida, 1868-1968.* Gainesville: University Presses of Florida.

McNamara, Patrick. 1968a. "Dynamics of the Catholic Church from pastoral to social concern." In The *Mexican American people,* edited by Leo Grebler, Ralph Guzmán, and Joan Moore. New York: Free Press.

_____. 1968b. "Protestants and Mexicans." In *The Mexican American people,* edited by Leo Grebler, Ralph Guzmán, and Joan Moore. New York: Free Press.

_____. 1968c. Social action priests in the Mexican American community. *Sociological Analysis* 2, 4: 177.

_____. 1973. "Catholicism, assimilation and the Chicano movement: Los Angeles as a case study." In *Chicanos and Native Americans,* edited by Rodolfo De La Garza, 124-130. Englewood Cliffs, NJ: Prentice-Hall.

_____. 1993. *Conscience first, tradition second: A study of young American Catholics.* Albany, NY: State University of New York Press.

_____. 1994. "Assumptions, theories and methods in the study of Latino religion after 25 years." In *Old masks, new faces: Religion and Latino identities,* edited by Anthony M. Stevens-Arroyo and Gilbert R. Cadena, 23-32. Vol. 2 of PARAL Studies Series. New York: Bildner Center Books.

Medina, Lara. 1994. Broadening the discourse at the theological table: An overview of Latino theology, 1968-1993. *Latino Studies Journal* 5, no. 3 (September): 10-35.

Meier, Matt S. 1976. "Mexican-Americans in the Southwest." In *Catholics in America: 1776-1976,* edited by R. Trisco, 107-110.

Mintz, Sidney. 1966. "Puerto Rico: An essay in the definition of national culture." In *Status of Puerto Rico: Selected Background Studies for the United States-Puerto Rico Commission on the Status of Puerto Rico.* Government Printing Office: Washington, DC. Reprinted, 1973, in *The Puerto Rican Experience,* edited by Francesco Cordasco and Eugene Bucchioni, 26-90. Totowa, NJ: Littlefield, Adams.

_____. 1974. *Worker in the cane: A Puerto Rican life history.* (1960) New York: W. W. Norton and Company.

Mirande, Alfredo. 1985. "The Church and the Chicano." In *The Chicano experience.* Notre Dame, IN: Notre Dame Press.

Mohr, Nicholasa. 1987. "Puerto Ricans in New York: Cultural evolution and identity." In *Images and identities: The Puerto Rican in two world contexts,* edited by Asela Rodriguez de Laguna. New Brunswick, NJ: Transaction Books.

Moore, Joan. 1980. "The death culture of Mexico and Mexican Americans." In *Death and dying,* edited by R. Kalish, 72-91. Farmingdale, NY: Baywood Publishing Co.

Morales, Cecilio J., Jr. 1984. Hispanics and other 'strangers': Implications of the new pastoral of the U.S. Catholic bishops. *Migration Today* 12, 1: 37-39.

Moran, Julio. 1983. "Latinos renewing bonds with religion." In *Southern California's Latino community* [A series of articles reprinted from the Los Angeles Times], edited by Jorge Ramos, 103-107. Los Angeles, CA: Los Angeles Times.

Mosher, William D., David P. Johnson, and Marjorie C. Horn. 1986. Religion and fertility in the United States: The importance of marriage pattern and Hispanic origin. *Demography* 23, no. 3 (August): 367-379.

Mosqueda, Lawrence J. 1986. *Chicanos, Catholicism, and political ideology.* Lanham, MD: University Press of America.

_____. 1990. Twentieth century Arizona, Hispanics, and the Catholic Church *U.S. Catholic Historian* 9, no. 1, 2 (Winter-Spring).

Nañez, Clotilde Falcón. 1981. "Hispanic clergy wives: Their contribution to United Methodism in the Southwest, later nineteenth century to the present." In *Women in new worlds,* edited by H. Thomas, 161-177. Nashville, TN: Abingdon.

Negrón de Montilla, Aída. 1976. *Americanization in Puerto Rico and the public school system, 1900-1930.* Río Piedras, PR: Editorial Universitaria.

Newman, Bernie S., and Peter G. Muzzonigro. 1993. The effects of traditional family values on the coming out process of gay male adolescents. *Adolescence* 28, no. 109 (Spring): 213-226.

Novo Peña, Silvia. 1993. "Religion." In *The Hispanic-American almanac,* edited by Nicolás Kanellos, 367-387. Detroit, MI: Gale Research, Inc.

Nyborg, Scott. 1991. Latin America Mission at Miami [case study]. *Urban Mission* 8 (March): 56-61.

Ortega y Medina, Juan A. 1986. "Race and democracy." In *Texas myths,* edited by Robert F. O'Connor, et al, 61-119. College Station: Texas A & M UP for Texas Commission for the Humanities.

Olson, James S. 1988. "The Hispanic Catholics." In *A Church of many cultures: Selected historical essays on ethnic American Catholicism,* edited by Dolores Liptack, 377-397. New York: Garland Publishing.

Ortiz, Carmen G., and Ena Vazquez Nuttall. 1987. Adolescent pregnancy: Effects of family support, education and religion on the decision to carry or terminate among Puerto Rican teenagers. *Adolescence* 22 (Winter): 897-917.

Ortiz, Isidro. 1984. Chicano urban politics and the politics of reform in the seventies. *Western Political Quarterly* 37, no. 4 (December): 564-577.

Ostling, Richard N. 1985. The crusade for Hispanic souls. *Time* 126, no. 1 (July): 78.

Padilla, Felix. 1987. *Puerto Rican Chicago.* Notre Dame, IN: University of Notre Dame Press.

Palmie, Stephan. 1986. Afro-Cuban religion in exile: Santería in south Florida. *Journal of Caribbean Studies* 5, no. 3 (Fall): 171-179.

Pantojas García, Emilio. 1979. *La iglesia protestante y la americanización de Puerto Rico, 1898-1917.* Bayamón, PR: PRISA.

Paz, Octavio. 1985. "Sons of La Malinche." In *The labyrinth of solitude,* 65-88. New York: Grove.

Peñalosa, Fernando, and Edward C. McDonagh. 1971. "Social mobility in a Mexican-American community." In *Chicanos: Social and psychological perspectives,* compiled by Nathaniel N. Wagner and Marsha J. Haug, 85-92. Saint Louis, MO: C.V. Mosby Co.

Pérez, Lisandro. 1994. "Cuban Catholics in the United States." In *Puerto Rican and Cuban Catholics in the U.S., 1900-1965,* edited by Jay P. Dolan and Jaime R. Vidal, 147-207. Notre Dame, IN: University of Notre Dame Press.

Pérez y González, María Elizabeth. 1993. *Latinas in ministry: A pioneering study of women ministers, educators and students of theology.* New York: New York City Mission Society.

_____. Forthcoming. "Caribbean women in a traditionally male-dominated institution—the church." In *Daughters of Calibán: Women in the 20th Century Caribbean,* edited by Consuelo López Springfield. Bloomington, IN: Indiana University Presss.

Pérez y Mena, Andrés I. 1977. Spiritualism as an adaptive mechanism among Puerto Ricans in the United States. *Cornell Journal of Social Relations* 12 (Fall): 125-136.

_____. 1989. Rites and wrongs. *Village Voice* (N.Y.) November 14.

_____. 1991. *Speaking with the dead: Development of Afro-Latin religion among Puerto Ricans in the United States.* New York: AMS Press.

_____. 1994. "Puerto Rican Spiritism as a transfeature of Afro-Latin religion." In *Enigmatic powers: Syncretism with African and Indigenous peoples' religions among Latinos,* edited by Anthony M. Stevens-Arroyo and Andrés I. Pérez y Mena, 137-155. Vol. 3 of PARAL Studies Series. New York: Bildner Center Books.

Piña, Michael. 1989. "The archaic, historical, and mythicized dimensions of Aztlán." In *Aztlán: Essays on the Chicano homeland,* edited by Rudolfo Anaya and Francisco Lomeli, 14- 48. Albuquerque, NM: University of New Mexico Press.

Plaskow, Judith, and Elizabeth Schussler Fiorenza, eds. 1992. Appropriation and reciprocity in womanist/mujerista/feminist work. *Journal of Feminist Studies in Religion* 8 (Fall): 91- 122.

Poblete, Renato, and Thomas F. O'Dea. 1960. Anomie and the 'quest for community': The formation of sects among the Puerto Ricans of New York. *The American Catholic Sociological Review* 21, no. 1: 18-36.

Polischuk, Pablo. 1990. "Hispanic Populations." In *Clergy Assessment and Career Development,* edited by Richard Hunt, et al, 154-157. Nashville, TN: Avingdon.

Ponce, Frank. 1985. "Religion and the State of Hispanic America." In *The State of Hispanic America.* Vol. 5. Oakland, CA: Hispanic Center for Advanced Policy Analysis.

Pulido, Alberto L. 1991a. Are you an emissary of Jesus Christ?: Justice, the Catholic church, and the Chicano movement. *Explorations in Ethnic Studies* 14, no. 1 (January): 17-34.

_____. 1991b. Nuestra Señora de Guadalupe: The Mexican Catholic experience in San Diego. *The Journal of San Diego History* 37, no. 4 (Fall): 237-254.

_____. 1993. "The religious dimension of Mexican Americans." In *A history of the Mexican American people,* 2d. ed., edited by Julian Samora, 223-234. Notre Dame, IN: University of Notre Dame Press.

_____. 1994a. Searching for the sacred: Conflict and struggle for Mexican Catholics in the Roman Catholic diocese of San Diego, 1936-1941. *Latino Studies Journal* 5, no. 3 (September): 37-59.

_____. 1994b. Presbiterianos mexicanos: Una perspectiva materialista de la religión y trabajo en el sur de Texas. *Cristianismo y Sociedad* 31-32, no. 118-119: 19-28.

Purdy, Beatrice A., et al. 1983. Religiosity, ethnicity, and mental health: Interface the 80s. *Counseling and Values* 27, no. 2 (January): 112-121.

Ramírez de Arellano, Annette B. and Conrad Seipp. 1983. *Colonialism, Catholicism and contraception: A history of birth control in Puerto Rico.* Chapel Hill, NC: University of North Carolina Press.

Ramírez, Ricardo. 1978a. The American church and Hispanic migration: An historical analysis (Part I). *Migration Today* 6, 1 (February): 16-20.

_____. 1978b. The American church and Hispanic migration: An historical analysis (Part II). *Migration Today* 6, 2 (April): 19-23.

_____. 1981. *Fiesta, worship and family.* San Antonio, Texas: Mexican American Cultural Center.

Reich, Alice Higman. 1979. "Ethnicity as a cultural system." In *Understanding religion and culture: Anthropological and theological perspectives,* edited by John H. Morgan, 195-215. Washington, D.C.: University Press of America.

Riley, Michael. 1992. Mexican American shrines in southern Arizona. *Journal of the Southwest* 2 (Summer): 206-231.

Rivera, Julius. 1978. Power and symbol in the Chicano movement. *Humanity and Society* 2, no. 1 (February): 1-17.

Rivera-Pagán, Luis N. 1994. "The penitential doctrine of restitution: Its use by Bartolomé de Las Casas to liberate popular religiosity during the conquest of America." In *An enduring flame: Studies on Latino popular religiosity,* edited by Anthony M. Stevens-Arroyo and Ana María Díaz- Stevens, 97-112. Vol. 1 of PARAL Studies Series. New York: Bildner Center Books.

Robiou Lamarche, Sebastián. 1970. *Manifiesto Ovni de Puerto Rico, Santo Domingo y Cuba.* San Juan, PR: Punto y Coma.

Rodríguez, Daniel R. 1986. *La primera evangelización norteamericana en Puerto Rico, 1898-1930.* New York: Ediciones Borinquen.

Rodríguez De Laguna, Asela, ed. 1987. *Images and identities: The Puerto Rican in two world contexts.* New Brunswick, NJ: Transaction Books.

Rodríguez, Jeanette. 1990. Hispanics and the sacred. *Chicago Studies* 29 (August): 137-154.

_____. 1994. *Our Lady of Guadalupe: Faith and empowerment among Mexican American women.* Austin: University of Texas Press.

Rodríguez, Josie. 1983. Mexican Americans: Factors influencing health practices. *Journal of School Health* 52, no. 2 (February): 136-139.

Rodriguez, Richard. 1982. "Credo." In *Hunger of memory.* Boston: Godine.

_____. 1986. *Evangélicos:* Changes of habit, changes of heart; the crusade for the soul of the mission. *Image Magazine* (October 26): 27-37.

Rodríguez, Sylvia. 1991. The Taos Pueblo Matachines: Ritual symbolism and interethnic relations. *American Ethnologist* 18 (May): 234-256.

Rogers, Mary Helen. 1987. The role of Our Lady of Guadalupe Parish in the adjustment of the Mexican community to life in the Indiana Harbor area, 1940-1951. In *Forging a community: The Latino experience in northwest Indiana, 1919-1975,* edited by James B. Lane and Edward J. Escobar, 187-200. Calumet, IL: Calumet Regional Archives and Cattails Press.

Rogler, Lloyd H. 1961. Puerto Rican spiritualist as a psychiatrist. *American Journal of Sociology* 67: 17-21. Reprinted, 1968, in *Puerto Rican children in mainland schools,* edited by Francesco Cordasco and Eugene Bucchioni, 55-61. Metuchen, NJ: The Scarecrow Press.

_____. 1972. *Migrant in the city: The life of a Puerto Rican action group.* New York: Basic Books.

Rogler, Lloyd, and August B. Hollingshead. 1965. *Trapped: Families and schizophrenia.* New York: John Wiley and Sons.

Romano, Octavio, ed. 1979. *Grito del sol.* Quarterly books. [Year four, Book One.] Berkeley: Quinto Sol.

Rosado, Caleb. 1992a. Ethnic labels confusing for all in politically correct world. *The Lumberjack* (April 8).

_____. 1992b. The role of liberation theology on the social identity of Latinos. *Latino Studies Journal* (Fall). Also published in *Religious meanings in modern times: New-Weberian studies in religion, society and culture,* edited by William H. Swatos. Lewiston, NY: Edwin Mellen Press.

_____. 1994. "The concept of Pueblo as a paradigm for explaining the religious experience of Latinos." In *Old masks, new faces: Religion and Latino identities,* edited by Anthony M. Stevens-Arroyo and Gilbert R. Cadena, 77-91. Vol. 2 of PARAL Studies Series. New York: Bildner Center Books.

Rosenhouse-Persson, Sandra, and Georges Sabagh. 1983. Attitudes toward abortion among Catholic Mexican-American women: The effects of religiosity and education. *Demography* 20, no. 1 (February): 87-98.

Ruiz, Pedro, and John Langrod. 1977. "The ancient art of folk healing: African influence in a New York City community mental health center." In *Traditional Healing,* edited by P. Singer, 80-95. Owerri, NY: Conch Magazine Ltd.

Sabagh, Georges, and David E. López. 1980. Religiosity and fertility: The case of Chicanas. *Social Forces* 59, no. 2 (December): 431-439.

Sánchez, Julio A. 1983. *The Community of the Holy Spirit: A movement of change in a convent of nuns in Puerto Rico.* Lanham, MD: University Press of America.

Sánchez Korrol, Virginia. 1988. In search of unconventional women: Histories of Puerto Rican women in religious vocations before mid-century. *Oral History Review* 16, no. 2 (Fall): 47-63.

Sandoval, Mercedes C. 1975. *La religión afrocubana.* Madrid: Ed. Playor.

_____. 1977. Afro-Cuban concepts of disease and its treatment in Miami. *Journal of Operational Psychiatry* 8, no. 2: 52-63.

_____. 1979. Santería as a mental health care system: An historical overview. *Social Science and Medicine* 13B, no. 2: 137-151.

_____. 1983. Santería. *The Journal of the Florida Medical Association* 7, no. 8: 620-628.

_____. 1994. "Afro-Cuban religion in perspective." In *Enigmatic powers: Syncretism with African and Indigenous peoples' religions among Latinos,* edited by Anthony M. Stevens-Arroyo and Andrés

I. Pérez y Mena, 81-98. Vol. 3 of PARAL Studies Series. New York: Bildner Center Books.

Sandoval, Moisés. 1978. The latinization of the Catholic Church. *Agenda* 8, no. 6 (November-December): 4-7.

_____. 1983. *Fronteras: A history of the Latin American church in the USA since 1513.* San Antonio: Mexican American Cultural Center.

_____. 1990. *On the move: A history of the Hispanic church in the United States.* New York: Orbis Books.

_____. 1992. "The church among the Hispanics in the United States." In *The church in Latin America, 1492-1992,* edited by Enrique Dussel, 230-242. Maryknoll, NY: Orbis Books.

_____. 1994. "The organization of a Hispanic church." In *Hispanic Catholic Culture in the U.S.: Issues and concerns,* edited by Jay P. Dolan and Allan Figueroa Deck, 131-165. Notre Dame, IN: University of Notre Dame Press.

Sandoval, Moisés, ed. 1983. *The Mexican American experience in the church: Reflections on identity and mission.* New York: Sadlier Books.

Santaella, P. Esteban. 1979. *Historia de los hermanos Cheo.* Santo Domingo, DR: Alfa y Omega.

Scarpetta, Olga. 1989. "Roles and relationships within the Puerto Rican family." In *Hispanics in New York: Religious, cultural and social experiences,* 2d ed., Vol. 2, edited by Olga Scarpetta and Ruth Doyle. New York: Office of Pastoral Research, Archdiocese of New York.

_____. 1989. "Religion, culture and gender - A comparative study of religious beliefs, attitudes and practices among 995 Hispanic men and women in the Archdiocese of New York." In *Hispanics in New York: Religious, cultural and social experiences,* 2d ed., Vol. 2, edited by Olga Scarpetta and Ruth Doyle. New York: Office of Pastoral Research, Archdiocese of New York.

Scarpetta, Olga, and Ruth Doyle. 1983. *Hispanics in New York: Who are we? Guide for reflection and dialogue.* New York: Office of Pastoral Research, Archdiocese of New York.

Schmidt, Adeny, and Amado M. Padilla. 1983. Grandparent-child interaction in a Mexican American group. *Hispanic Journal of Behavioral Sciences* 5, no. 2 (June): 191-198.

Seda Bonilla, Eduardo. 1973. *Social change and personality in a Puerto Rican agrarian reform community.* Evanston, IL: Northwestern University Press.

Siefken, Stephanie. 1993. The Hispanic perspective on death and dying: A combination of respect, empathy and spirituality. Pride Institute-*Journal of Long Term Home Health Care* 12, no. 2 (Spring): 26-28.

Silva, Milton, et al. 1984. Puerto Ricans of Hawaii: Immigrants and migrants. *Hispanic Journal of Behavioral Sciences* 6, no. 1 (March): 33-52.

Silva-Gotay, Samuel. 1971. La iglesia y la pobreza en Puerto Rico. (Análisis socio-político de la historia del protestantismo en Puerto Rico.) *Revista de Administración Pública,* Universidad de Puerto Rico, 4, no. 2.

_____. 1983a. La religión y la cultura puertorriqueña. *Homines* (Universidad Interamericana). (January).

_____. 1983b. "La iglesia protestante como agente de americanización en Puerto Rico, 1898-1917." In *Politics, society and culture in the Caribbean,* edited by Blanca Silvestrini. San Juan: Universidad de Puerto Rico.

_____. 1985a. "Social history of the churches in Puerto Rico, preliminary notes, 1509-1980." In *Towards a history of the church in the Third World: The issue of periodization.* Geneve, Switzerland: EATWT.

_____. 1985b. La iglesia católica en el proceso político de la americanización de Puerto Rico, 1898-1930. *Cristianismo y Sociedad* 23, no. 86 (3ra. época): 7-34.

_____. 1985c. La iglesia católica en el proceso político de la americanización en Puerto Rico, 1898-1930. *Revista de Historia* 1, no. 1 (January-June): 102-120, and Vol. 1, no. 2 (Julio-Diciembre): 168-187.

_____. 1990. Desarrollo de la dimensión religiosa del nacionalismo en Puerto Rico: 1898-1989. *Estudios Interdisciplinarios de América Latina* (Revista Escuela de Historia de la Universidad de Tel Aviv, Israel) 1, no. 1 (Enero-Junio): 59-82.

_____. 1994a. "On the question of a "scientific history" for the Latino church." In *Hidden stories: Unveiling the history of the Latino church,* 23-47. Decatur, GA: AETH.

_____. 1994b. "The ideological dimensions of popular religiosity and cultural identity in Puerto Rico." In *An enduring flame: Studies on Latino popular religiosity,* edited by Anthony M. Stevens-Arroyo and Ana María Díaz-Stevens, 133- 170. Vol. 1 of PARAL Studies Series. New York: Bildner Center Books.

Skansie, Juli Ellen. 1985. *Death is for all: Death and death related beliefs of rural Spanish-Americans.* New York: AMS Press.

Sosa, Juan J. 1983. *Popular religiosity and religious syncretism: Santeria and Spiritism.* Miami: Documentaciones Sureste.

Soto, Antonio R. 1979. The Church in California and the Chicano: A sociological analysis. *El Grito del Sol* 4, no. 1 (Winter): 47-74.

Steele, Thomas J. 1982. *Santos and saints: The religious folk art of Hispanic New Mexico.* Santa Fe, NM: Ancient City Press.

Steiner, Stan. 1969. "The unfrocked priests." In *La Raza: The Mexican Americans.* New York: Harper Colopmon.

Stevens-Arroyo, Anthony M. 1974a. "Religion and the Puerto Ricans in New York." In *Puerto Rican Perspectives,* edited by E. Mapp, 119-130. New Jersey: Scarecrow Press.

_____. 1974b. The Puerto Ricans on the mainland. *Migration Today* 2, no. 3 (Summer): 4ff.

_____. 1976a. Migration, ethnicity and liberation theology. *Migration Today* 4, no. 3 (June): 7.

_____. 1976b. The American Catholic Church faces ethnicity and migration. *Migration Today* 4, no. 5 (December): 9.

_____. 1977. Marxism and the Hispanic movements of the United States. *New Catholic World* 220 (May/June): 126-128.

_____. 1980a. What is the ethnicity of the American Church? [from *The Priest,* November 1976: 37-41]. Excerpted, 1980, in *Prophets denied honor,* edited by Antonio M. Stevens- Arroyo, 352-357. Maryknoll, NY: Orbis Books.

_____. 1980b. "Puerto Rican struggles in the Catholic Church." In *The Puerto Rican struggle: Essays on survival in the United States,* edited by C. Rodríguez, V. Sánchez Korrol and J. O. Alers, 129-139. Maplewood, NJ: Waterfront Press.

_____. 1983. "Puerto Rican migration to the United States." In *Fronteras: A history of Hispanic Catholics in the U.S.A. since 1513,* edited by Moisés Sandoval, 269-276. San Antonio: Mexican American Cultural Center.

_____. 1984. A Taino tale: A mythological statement of social order. *Caribbean Review* 13, no. 4 (Fall): 24-26.

_____. 1988. *The cave of the Jagua: The mythological world of the Tainos.* Albuquerque, NM: University of New Mexico Press.

_____. 1989. The radical shift in the Spanish approach to intercivilizational encounter. *Comparative Civilizations Review* 21 (Fall): 80-101.

_____. 1990. Puerto Rico's future status: Prisoners of many myths. *The Nation* 250, no. 3 (January 22): 86-90.

_____. 1992. "Catholic ethos as politics: The Puerto Rican nationalists." In *Neo-Weberian studies in society and religion,* edited by William Swatos, 172-193. Lewiston, NY: Edwin Mellen Press.

_____. 1993. The Inter-Atlantic paradigm: The failure of Spanish medieval colonialism of the Canary and Caribbean Islands. *Comparative Studies in Society and History* 35, no. 3 (July): 515-543.

_____. 1994a. "The persistence of religious perception in an alien world." In *Enigmatic powers: Syncretism with African and Indigenous peoples' religions among Latinos,* edited by Anthony M. Stevens-Arroyo and Andrés I. Pérez y Mena, 113- 135. Vol. 3 of PARAL Studies Series. New York: Bildner Center Books.

_____. 1994b. "The emergence of a social identity among Latino Catholics: An appraisal." In *Hispanic Catholic culture in the U.S.: Issues and concerns,* edited by Jay P. Dolan and Allan Figueroa Deck, 77-130. Vol. 3 of the Notre Dame series on the history of Catholicism among Hispanics. Notre Dame: University of Notre Dame Press.

_____. 1994c. "How Latino/Hispanic identity becomes a religious reality." In *Yearbook of American and Canadian churches,* edited by Kenneth Bedell, 5-6. Nashville: Abingdon Press.

_____. 1995. Latino Catholicism and the eye of the beholder: Notes towards a new sociological paradigm. *Latino Studies Journal* 6, no. 2 (May): 22-55.

Stevens-Arroyo, Anthony M., ed. 1980. *Prophets denied honor: An anthology of the Hispanic church in the United States.* Maryknoll, New York: Orbis Books.

Stevens-Arroyo, Anthony M., and Ana Maria Díaz-Stevens. 1993. "Latino churches and school as urban battlegrounds." In *Handbook of urban schooling in America,* edited by Stanley Rothstein. Westport, CT: Greenwood Press.

_____. 1994. "Religious faith and institutions in the forging of Latino identities." In *Handbook of Hispanic cultures in the United States,* edited by Félix Padilla, 257-291. Houston: Arte Público Press.

Stevens-Arroyo, Anthony M., and Ana María Díaz-Stevens, eds. 1994. *An enduring flame: Studies in Latino popular religiosity.* New York: Bildner Center Books.

Stevens-Arroyo, Anthony M., and Andrés I. Pérez y Mena, eds. 1995. *Enigmatic powers: Syncretism with African and Indigenous peoples' religions among Latinos.* New York: Bildner Center Books.

Stevens-Arroyo, Anthony M., and Gilbert R. Cadena, eds. 1995. *Old masks, new faces: Religion and Latino identities.* New York: Bildner Center Books.

Sullivan, Patrick J., C.S.C. 1987a. "Braceros and migrants," "Earlier Chávez and farmworkers, 1960's," and "Later Chávez and farmworkers, 1970's." In *Blue collar, Roman collar, white collar: U.S. Catholic involvement in labor management controversies, 1960-1980,* 1-171. Lanham: University Press of America.

Sumner, Margaret L. 1963. Mexican-American Minority Churches, U.S.A. *Practical Anthropology* 10, no. 3 (May-June). Reprinted, 1970, in *Mexican-Americans in the United States: A reader,* edited by John H. Burma, 225-233. New York: Schenkman Publishing Company.

Sutton, Constance R., and Elsa M. Chaney, eds. 1987. *Caribbean life in New York City: Sociocultural dimensions.* New York: Center for Migration Studies.

Teichner, Victor J., James J. Cadden, and Gail W. Berry. 1981. The Puerto Rican patient: Some historical, cultural and psychological aspects. *Journal of the American Academy of Psychoanalysis* 9, no. 2 (April): 277-289.

Thompson, John. 1994. Santo Niño de Atocha. *Journal of the Southwest* 1 (Spring): 1-18.

Torres, Eliseo. 1983. "Niño Fidencio, and Teresita." In *The folk healer: The Mexican american tradition of curanderismo,* 41-54. Kingsville, TX: Nieves Press.

Traba, Marta. 1972. *La rebelión de los santos.* Río Piedras, PR: Ediciones Puerto.

Treviño, Roberto R. 1994. In their own way: Parish funding and Mexican American ethnicity in Catholic Houston, 1911-1972. *Latino Studies Journal* 5, no. 3 (September): 87-107.

Trotter, Robert T., and Juan Antonio Chavira. 1981. "The history of curanderismo, and curanderos' theories of healing." In *Curanderismo: Mexican American folk healing,* 61-71. Athens: University of Georgia Press.

Tumin, Melvin M. and Arnold S. Feldman. 1955. The miracle at Sabana Grande. *Public Opinion Quarterly* 19: 2. Reprinted, 1972, in *Portrait of a Society,* edited by Eugenio Fernández Méndez, 356-369. San Juan: University of Puerto Rico Press.

Turner, Kay F. 1982. Mexican American home altars: Towards their interpretation. *Aztlan* 13, no. 1, 2 (Spring-Fall): 309-326.

_____. 1991. "Because of this photography: The making of a Mexican folk saint." In *El Niño Fidencio: A heart thrown open,* 120-135. Santa Fe: Museum of New Mexico Press.

Urdaneta, María Luisa. 1979. "Flesh pots, faith, or finances? Fertility rates among Mexican Americans." In *The Chicano Experience,* edited by Stanley A. West and June Macklin, 191-206. Boulder, CO: Westview Press.

Valdez, Daniel T. 1973. Los padres: Hispano priests organize. *La Luz* 2, no. 2 (May).

Vidal, Jaime R. 1994a. "Towards an understanding of synthesis in Iberian and Hispanic American popular religiosity." In *An enduring flame: Studies on Latino popular religiosity,* edited by Anthony M. Stevens-Arroyo and Ana María Díaz- Stevens, 69-96. Vol. 1 of PARAL Studies Series. New York: Bildner Center Books.

_____. 1994b. "Citizens yet strangers: The Puerto Rican experience." In *Puerto Rican and Cuban Catholics in the U.S., 1900-1965,* edited by Jay P. Dolan and Jaime R. Vidal, 11-146. Notre Dame, IN: University of Notre Dame Press.

Vidal, Teodoro. 1974. *Los milagros.* San Juan, PR: Editorial Alba.

_____. 1989. *Tradiciones en la brujería puertorriqueña.* San Juan, PR: Ediciones Alba.

Vidaurri, Cynthia L. 1991. "Texas-Mexican religious folk art in Robstown, Texas." In *Hecho en Texas: Texas-Mexican folk arts and crafts,* edited by Joe S. Graham, 222-249. Denton: University of North Texas Press.

Wagner, Roland M. 1987. Changes in extended family relationships for Mexican Americans and Anglo single mothers. *Journal of Divorce* 11 (Winter): 69-87.

Wakefield, Dan. 1959. *Island in the City: The World of Spanish Harlem.* Boston, MA: Houghton Mifflin.

Weber, Francis J. 1970. Irish Born Champion of the Mexican Americans. *California Historical Society Quarterly* 49, no. 3 (September): 233-249.

Weigert, Andrew, William D'Antonio, and Arthur Rubel. 1971. Protestantism and assimilation among Mexican-Americans: An exploratory study of ministers' reports. *Journal for the Scientific Study of Religion* 10 (Fall): 219-232.

Weigle, Martha. 1970. *The Penitentes of the Southwest.* Santa Fe: Ancient City Press.

Weyr, Thomas. 1988. "Religion." In *Hispanic U.S.A.: Breaking the melting pot,* 190-218. New York: Harper and Row.

Wodarski, John S. 1992. "Social work practice with Hispanic Americans." In *Cultural diversity and social work practice,* edited by Dianne F. Harrison, John Wodarski, and Bruce A. Thyer, 71-105. Springfield, IL: Charles C. Thomas, Publisher.

Wolf, Eric. 1972. "The Virgin of Guadalupe: A Mexican national symbol" in *Readings in comparative religion: An anthropological approach,* edited by William A. Lessa and Evon A. Vogt, 149-153. New York: Harper and Row.

Zaragoza, Edward C. 1990. The Santiago Apostol of Loiza, Puerto Rico. *Caribbean Studies* 23: 125-139.

Zayas Micheli, Luis O. 1990. *Catolicismo popular en Puerto Rico: una explicación sociológica.* Río Piedras, PR: Editorial Raices.

Religious Writings, and Theological and Related Publications

II

Abalos, David T. 1989. "Latino case studies." In *Hispanics in New York: Religious, cultural and social experiences,* 2d ed., Vol. 1, edited by Ruth Doyle and Olga Scarpetta. New York: Office of Pastoral Research, Archdiocese of New York.

Acevedo Delgado, Germán. 1988. Hispanic community has reason to celebrate. *Christian Social Action* 1 (July-August): 26.

Acosta, Samuel. 1989. The Hispanic Council of the United Church of Christ: Its history, impact, and ability to motivate policy. *Chicago Theological Seminary Register* 79 (Summer): 28-41.

Acosta, Sam, Lucille Groh, Gustavo Hernández, and Barbara Rathbone. 1990. Counseling Hispanics in the United States. *The Journal of Pastoral Care* 44 (Spring): 33-41.

Aquino, María Pilar. 1992. "Perspectives on a Latina's feminist liberation theology." In *Frontiers of Hispanic theology,* edited by A. Figueroa Deck, 23-40. Maryknoll, NY: Orbis Books.

_____. 1993. Directions and foundations of Hispanic/Latino theology: Toward a Mestiza theology of liberation. *Journal of Hispanic/Latino Theology* 1, no. 1: 5-21.

Aragón, Rafael J. 1982. La realidad histórica y existencial del advenimiento de Jesucristo. *Apuntes: Reflexiones Teológicas Desde el Margen Hispano* 2, no. 4 (Winter): 85-88.

Arias, Pedro. 1970. Católicos por La Raza: Open letter to Cardinal McIntyre. *La Raza* 1, no. 2: 49-52.

_____. 1972. Bautizar: Gran negocio de algunos curas. *La Raza* 1, no. 8 (April): 10-11.

Armendáriz, Rubén P. 1982. Estad pues firmes: Estudio bíblico. *Apuntes: Reflexiones Teológicas desde el Margen Hispano* 2, no. 2 (Summer): 27-30.

_____. 1983. The preparation of Hispanics for the ministry of the church. *Theological Education* 20 (Autumn): 53-57.

_____. 1988. Las posadas. *Reformed Liturgy and Music* 22, no. 3 (Summer): 142-143.

Arzube, Juan. 1977. Illegal aliens: Refugees from hunger. *La Raza* 3, no. 2 (Summer): 11-14.

_____. 1980. "Multi-Hispanic urban solidarity." In *Prophets denied honor,* edited by Antonio M. Stevens-Arroyo, 284-286. Maryknoll, NY: Orbis Books.

Atkinson, Ernest E. 1983. Hispanic worship patterns in San Antonio, Texas. *Austin Seminary Bulletin* 98 (April): 11-18.

Austin, Tom. 1991. Let the church bells ring mariachi. *The Other Side* 27 (March-April): 46-47.

Aymes, María de la Cruz. 1987. "Toward the fulfillment of a dream." In *Faith and culture: A multicultural catechetical resource,* edited by A. Peláez, 65-76. Washington, D.C.: Department of Education, United States Catholic Conference.

Bacalski-Martínez, Roberto R. 1979. "Aspects of Mexican American cultural heritage." In *The Chicanos: As we see ourselves,* edited by Arnulfo D. Trejo, 19-35. Tucson, AZ: University of Arizona Press.

Bañuelas, Arturo, ed. 1991. U.S. Hispanic Roman Catholic theology: a bibliography. *Apuntes* 11 (Winter):93-103.

_____. 1992. U.S. Hispanic theology. *Missiology* 20 (April): 275-300.

Barron, Clemente. 1990. On my mind: Racism and vocations. *New Theology Review* 3, no. 4 (November):92-103.

Barron, Mario, CSJ. 1976. "Chicano struggle." In *Theology in the Americas,* edited by Sergio Torres and John Eagleson, 207-212. Maryknoll, NY: Orbis Books.

Basso, Teresita. 1978. "Ministry to Hispano Mexicano/Chicano youth." In *Resources for youth ministry,* edited by Michael Warren, 190-201. New York: Paulist Press.

Benavides, Albert. 1979. "An experience of a large urban Mexican American parish." In *Becoming a Catholic Christian,* edited by W. Reedy, 66-74. New York: Sadlier.

Boehm, Mike. 1986. Musical resources for the Hispanic community. *Pastoral Music* 10, no. 3 (February-March): 24- 25.

Borges, Haydee. 1980. "The voice of the lay woman in the Church of the Northeast of the United States of America." In *Prophets denied honor,* edited by Antonio M. Stevens-Arroyo, 289-291. Maryknoll, NY: Orbis Books.

Brackenridge, R. Douglas, and Francisco O. Garcia-Treto. 1977. Presbyterians and Mexican Americans: From paternalism to partnership. *Journal of Presbyterian History* 55 (Summer): 161-178.

Breiter, Toni. 1977a. Hispanics and the Roman Catholic Church. *Agenda* 7, no. 1 (January-February): 4-9.

_____. 1977b. Hispanic voices being heard, being heeded? *Agenda* 7, no. 5 (September-October): 23-25.

Buckley, Francis. 1991. Popular religiosity and sacramentality: Learning from Hispanics a deeper sense of symbol, ritual, and sacrament. *Living Light* 27, no. 4 (Summer): 351-360.

Bunnell, Robert. 1984. Competition for Latino souls: A Catholic perspective. *Nuestro* 8, no. 1 (January-February): 32-34.

Burciaga, José Antonio. 1986. In celebration of a man's ecumenism. *Vista* 2, no. 4 (December): 26.

Burns, Jeffrey M. 1987. "Building the best: A history of Catholic parish life in the Pacific states." In *The American Catholic parish,* Vol. 2, edited by Jay P. Dolan, 7- 135. New York: Paulist Press.

Cadena, Gilbert R., and Lara Medina. Forthcoming. "Liberation theology and social change: Chicanas and Chicanos in the Catholic church." In *Chicanas and Chicanos in contemporary society: Explorations in culture, politics and society,* edited by Robert de Anda. New York: MacMillan.

Cantero, Araceli M. 1991. Católicos hispanos alcanzan 'mayoría de edad'. *La Voz Católica,* January 31.

Carrillo, Alberto. 1980. "Toward a national Hispano church." In *Prophets denied honor,* edited by Antonio M. Stevens- Arroyo, 154-157. Maryknoll, NY: Orbis Books.

Castuera, Ignacio. 1975. The theology and practice of liberation in the Mexican American context. *Perkins Journal of Theology* 29 (Fall): 2-11.

Chambers, Edward. 1977. The church: The best hope for change and social justice. *La Raza* 3, no. 2 (Summer): 45-47.

Chávez, Angélico, Fr. 1980. "Native Hispano vocations." In *Prophets denied honor,* edited by Antonio M. Stevens-Arroyo, 77-79. Maryknoll, NY: Orbis Books.

_____. 1981. *But time and chance: The story of Padre Martínez of Taos: 1793-1867.* Santa Fe, NM: Sunstone Press.

_____. 1985. *Tres macho—he said: Padre Gallegos of Albuquerque, New Mexico's first congressman.* Santa Fe, NM: William Gannon.

Chávez, Tomás, Jr. 1983. Quinceañera: A liturgy in the Reformed tradition. *Austin Seminary Bulletin:* Faculty Edition 98 (April): 34-47.

_____. 1986. The theological basis for a 'serviglesia'. *Apuntes: Reflexiones Teológicas desde el Margen Hispano* 6, no. 2 (Summer): 44-47.

Church vs. Católicos. 1969. *La raza* 1, no. 1: 19-22.

Coca, Benjamín. 1977. *El ermitaño y otras historias religiosas del Norte.* New Mexico: Montezuma.

Collinson-Streng, Paul, and Ismael de la Tejera. 1986. "Bible and mission in a Hispanic congregation." In *Bible and Mission,* edited by Wayne Stumme, 129-137. Minneapolis, MI: Ausburg Publishing House.

Costas, Orlando E. 1986. "Social justice in the other Protestant tradition: A Hispanic perspective." In *Contemporary ethical issues,* edited by F. Greenspahn, 205- 229. Hoboken, NJ: Ktav; [Denver, CO]: Center for Jewish Studies at the University of Denver.

_____. 1988. "Survival, hope, and liberation in the other American church: An Hispanic case study." In *One faith, many cultures,* edited by R. Costa, 136-144. Vol. 2 of Boston Theological Institute Annual Series.

_____. 1989. Conversion as a complete experience: A Hispanic case study. *Latin American Pastoral Issues* 14, no. 1: 8-32.

_____. 1992. "Hispanic theology in North America." In *Struggles for solidarity: Liberation theologies in tension,* edited by Lorine Getz and Ruy Costa, 63-74. Minneapolis, MN: Fortress.

Curl, R.F. 1951. *Southwest Texas Methodism.* Inter-Board Council, Southwest Texas Conference.

Curti, Josafat. 1975. The Chicano and the church: Dominant Anglo institutions demand cultural suicide and self-negation as the price for Chicano's acceptance. *The Christian Century* 92 (March 12): 253-257.

Davis, Kenneth G. 1989. One hundred and twenty five years of Hispanic presence in California church. *East Bay Monitor* (July): 9
_____. 1990. Base communities: Changing the chemistry of the church. *The Catholic World* 233 (November-December): 281-285.
_____. 1991a. On being a frog in my field. *The Priest* 47, no. 10 (October): 6-7.
_____. 1991b. CORHIM Hispanic Seminars. *Review for Religious.* (November- December): 881-887.
_____. 1992a. Preaching in Spanish as a second language. *Homiletic* (Fall): 7-10.
_____. 1992b. A return to the roots: Conversion and the culture of the Mexican-descent Catholic. *Pastoral Psychology* 40, no. 3 (January): 139-158.
_____. Forthcoming. "Inculturation and missiology." In *Theologizing for a renewed society,* edited by Margo LeBert. Mahwah, NJ: Paulist Press.
Díaz, Frank. 1987. Looking at Hispanic ministry in 1987. *Austin Seminary Bulletin:* Faculty Edition 103 (October): 37- 42.
Díaz, Rey. 1989. La liberación hispana en U.S.A. *Apuntes: Reflexiones Teológicas desde el Margen Hispano* 9 (Spring): 13-15.
Díaz-Stevens, Ana María, ed. 1974. *Una comunidad de mujeres.* New York: United Methodist Church.
_____. 1975. *Diversos dones, un espíritu.* New York: United Methodist Church.
_____. 1976. *Nuestro mundo será lo que nosotros seamos.* New York: United Methodist Church.
_____. 1977. *Ustedes serán mis testigos.* New York: United Methodist Church.
Díaz-Stevens, Ana María, and Antonio M. Stevens-Arroyo. 1980. The Hispano model of church: A people on the march. *New Catholic World* (July-August): 153-157.
Dimas Soberal, José. 1988. *La verdad sobre ciertos ministerios falsos.* Bayamón, Puerto Rico: Grafar Arte.
_____. 1989a. *Madres solteras.* Bayamón, Puerto Rico: Grafar Arte.
_____. 1989b. *La verdad sobre la ex-monja Ilduara Pabón Agudelo.* Bayamón, Puerto Rico: Grafar Arte.
Doyle, Janet. 1983. Escoja educación católica! *Momentum* 14, no. 1 (February): 37-38.

Duarte, E.B. 1972. Spanish speaking Catholics call for more Hispano bishops. *Agenda* 2, no. 2 (August): 16-18.

Dussel, Enrique. 1976. "A Latin American people in the United States." In *History and the theology of liberation*. New York: Orbis Books.

Elford, George. 1983. Catholic schools and bilingual education. *Momentum* 14, no. 1 (February): 35-37.

Elizondo, Virgil. 1968. *Educación religiosa para el méxico-norteamericano*. Catequesis Latinoamericana [México].

_____. 1974. Biblical pedagogy of evangelization. *American Ecclesiastical Review* 168, no. 8 (October).

_____. 1975a. "Pastoral planning for the Spanish speaking in the United States." In *Colección Mestiza*. San Antonio: Mexican American Cultural Center.

_____. 1975b. "A challenge to theology: The situation of Hispanic Americans." In *Proceedings of the Catholic Theological Society of America* 30: 163-176

_____. 1975c. A theological interpretation of the Mexican American experience. *Perkins Journal of Theology* 29 (Fall): 12-21.

_____. 1975d. *Christianity and culture*. Hunington: Our Sunday Visitor.

_____. 1976a. "The situation of Hispanic Americans: A people twice conquered; twice colonized; twice oppressed." In *El Quetzal emplumece,* compiled by Carmela Montalvo and Leonardo Anguiano, 339-349. San Antonio, TX: Mexican American Cultural Center.

_____. 1976b. The San Antonio experiment. *New Catholic World* (May-June): 117-120.

_____. 1977a. Our Lady of Guadalupe as a cultural symbol: The power of the powerless. *Concilium* 102, edited by Herman Schmidt and David Power. New York: Crossroads.

_____. 1977b. *The human quest: A search for meaning through life and death*. Hunington: Our Sunday Visitor.

_____. 1978. *Mestizaje: The dialectic of birth and gospel*. San Antonio: Mexican American Cultural Center.

_____. 1979a. "Who is the cathecumen in the Spanish speaking community of the U.S.A?" In *Becoming a Catholic Christian*, edited by William J. Reedy. New York: Sadlier.

_____. 1979b. Theological education and liberation theology: A symposium, response to Frederick Herzog. *Theological Education* 16, no. 1 (Autumn): 34-37.

_____. 1980a. Identity and mission of Hispanic (USA) Catholics. *Origins.*

_____. 1980b. "Pastoral planning for the Spanish-speaking in the United States of America." In *Prophets denied honor,* edited by Antonio M. Stevens-Arroyo, 183-187. Maryknoll, NY: Orbis Books.

_____. 1980c. *La Morenita: Evangelizer of the Americas.* San Antonio, TX: Mexican American Cultural Center.

_____. 1981a. A bicultural approach to religious education. *The Journal of the Religious Education Association* 76 (May- June): 258-270.

_____. 1981b. The Hispanic church in the U.S.A: A local ecclesiology. *Proceedings of the Catholic Theological Society of America* 36: 155-170.

_____. 1981c. "The gospel mandate: Implications for the future." In *Proceedings of the National Catholic Educators Association Curriculum Conference,* 18-28.

_____. 1982. A report on racism: A Mexican American in the United States. *Concilium* 151, 1: 61-66. Also published, 1982, in *The church and racism,* edited by G. Baum and J. Coleman, 61-65. New York: Seabury Press.

_____. 1983a. "Toward an American-Hispanic theology of liberation in the U.S.A." In *Irruption of the Third World,* edited by Virginia Fabella and Sergio Torres, 50-55. New York: Orbis Books.

_____. 1983b. *Galilean journey: The Mexican American promise.* New York: Orbis Books.

_____. 1983c. *Virgen y madre: Reflexiones bíblicas sobre María de Nazaret.* San Antonio: Mexican American Cultural Center.

_____. 1983d. *¿Quién eres tu?* San Antonio: Mexican American Cultural Center.

_____. 1983e. "By their fruits you will know them: The biblical roots of peace and justice." In *Education for peace and justice,* edited by Padraic O'Hare, 39-65. San Francisco: Harper and Row.

_____. 1983f. "Theological and biblical foundations for comunidades de base." In *Developing basic Christian communities.* Chicago Federation of Priests' Councils.

_____. 1983g. Christian challenge and the disadvantaged. *Linacre Quarterly* 51 (August): 242-245.

_____. 1985. Self-affirmation of the Hispanic church. *The Ecumenist* (March-April).

_____. 1986a. Popular religion as support of identity: A pastoral-psychological case-study based on the Mexican American experience in the U.S.A. *Concilium* 186, 4: 36-43.

_____. 1986b. "Popular religion as support of identity: A pastoral-psychological case-study based on the Mexican experience in the U.S.A." In *Popular religion,* edited by N. Greinacher and N. Mette, 36-43. Edinburgh, Scotland: T & T Clark.

_____. 1987a. "Hispanic evangelization: A lost cause?" In *Paulist Evangelization Association.*

_____. 1987b. "The ministry of the church and contemporary migration." In *Social Thought:* Special Papal Edition (January). Washington, D.C.

_____. 1987c. "The Mexican American religious education experience." In *Ethnicity in the education of the church,* edited by C. Foster, 75-89. Nashville, TN: Scarritt Press.

_____. 1988a. America's changing face. *The Tablet* (London), July 23.

_____. 1988b. *The future is mestizo: Life where cultures meet.* Oak Park [IL]: Meyer-Stone.

_____. 1989a. "Mestizaje as locus of theological reflection." In *The future of liberation theology,* edited by Marc Ellis and Otto Maduro, 358-374. New York: Orbis Books.

_____. 1989b. Elements for a Mexican American mestizo christology. *Christologies in Encounter* 15, no. 2. Voices From the Third World. Sri Lanka (December).

_____. 1989c. "Mary and evangelization in the Americas." In *Mary: Woman of Nazareth,* edited by Doris Donnelly, 146-160. New York: Paulist Press.

_____. 1993. Hispanic theology and popular piety: From interreligious encounter to a new ecumenism. *Proceedings of the Catholic Theological Society of America* 48: 1-14.

Elizondo, Virgil P., and John Linskens. 1975. Pentecost and pluralism. *Momentum* (October): 12-15.

Elizondo, Virgil P., and Norbert Greinacher, eds. 1980. *Women in a man's church.* Edinburgh, Scotland: T & T Clark.

_____. 1981. *Tensions between the church of the First World and of the Third World.* Edinburgh, Scotland: T & T Clark.

Erdman, Daniel. 1983. Liberation and identity: Indo-Hispano youth. *Religious Education* 78 (Winter): 76-89.

Escamilla, Roberto. 1977. Worship in the context of Hispanic culture. *Worship* 51 (July): 290-293.

Espín, Orlando O. 1988. "The sources of Hispanic theology." In *Proceedings of the Forty-Third Annual Convention, CTSA* [Toronto], 43: 122-125.

_____. 1989. " 'Lilies of the field': A Hispanic theology of providence and human responsibility." In *Proceedings of the Forty-Fourth Annual Convention, CTSA* [St. Louis], 44: 70- 90.

_____. 1991. "The vanquished, faithful solidarity and the Marian symbol: A Hispanic perspective on providence." In *On keeping providence,* edited by Joan Coultas and Barbara Doherty, 84-101. Terre Haute, IN: St. Mary of the Woods Press.

_____. 1992a. "Grace and humanness: A Hispanic perspective." In *We are a people! Initiatives in Hispanic American theology,* edited by Roberto Goizueta, 133-164. Minneapolis, MN: Fortress Press.

_____. 1992b. The God of the vanquished: Foundations for a latino spirituality. *Listening* 27, no. 1 (Winter): 70-84.

_____. 1993. Hispanic/Latino theology. *Proceedings of the Catholic Theological Society of America* 48: 89.

_____. 1994. "Popular Catholicism among Latinos." In *Hispanic Catholic culture in the U.S.: Issues and concerns,* edited by Jay P. Dolan and Allan Figueroa Deck, 308-359. Notre Dame, IN: University of Notre Dame Press.

Espín, Orlando, and Sixto J. Garcia. 1987. "Hispanic-American theology." In *Proceedings of the Forty-Second Annual Convention, CTSA* [Philadelphia], 42: 114-119.

Espinoza, H.O. 1990. "Response to William H. Bentley ['Reflections on the scope and function of black evangelical theology', 299 333]." In *Evangelical affirmations,* edited by K. Kantzer and C. Henry, 335-342. Grand Rapids, MI: Academie Books.

Estrada, Rey. 1988. The path to sainthood. *Vista* 4, no. 3 (September): 6.

Everia, Angela. 1975. *A new direction for catechetics and liturgy for the Mexican American.* San Antonio, TX: Mexican American Cultural Center.

_____. 1977. Cultura y fe relacionadas a educación religiosa. *El Visitante Dominical* (September 11).

_____. 1979. Death and funerals in the Mexican American community. *PACE* 10.

_____. 1984. Particular characteristics towards a 'pastoral hispana'. *Apuntes: Reflexiones Teológicas desde el Margen Hispano* 4, no. 1 (Spring): 11-13.

_____. 1989. Quince años: Celebrating a tradition. *Catechist* (March): 10-11.

_____. 1991. Religión casera: The Hispanic way. *Momentum* 22, no. 4 (November): 32-34.

Fernández Zayas, Marcelo. 1989. Los bautizos: Lo que pasa a los hispanos en USA. *Réplica* 20 (November): 16.

Figueroa Deck, Allan S. J. 1976. Liturgy and Mexican American culture. *Modern Liturgy* 3, no. 7 (October): 24-26.

_____. 1978. A Christian perspective on the reality of illegal immigration. *Social Thought* (Fall): 39-53.

_____. 1979. Una perspectiva cristiana sobre la inmigración ilegal. *Christus*.

_____. 1981. A Hispanic perspective on Christian family life. *America* 145, no. 20 (December 19): 400-402.

_____. 1983a. El movimiento hispano y la iglesia católica de los Estados Unidos. *Christus* (March): 48-50.

_____. 1983b. Vida familiar cristiana: Perspectivas hispanas. *Christus* (March): 44-47.

_____. 1986a. Hispanic vocations: Light at the end of the tunnel. *Call to Growth Ministry* 11, no. 2 (Winter): 12-18.

_____. 1986b. Hispanic vocations: What happens once you've got them. *The Priest* (March): 18-22.

_____. 1986c. Rural Hispanic ministry. *Rural Roots* 5, no. 1 (May/June).

_____. 1986d. Hispanic ministry comes of age. *America* 154, no. 19 (May 17): 400-402.

_____. 1987. Ministry and vocations: Going back to the drawing board. *America* 156, no. 10 (March 14): 212-218.

_____. 1989a. *The second wave: Hispanic ministry and the evangelization of cultures*. New York: Paulist Press.

_____. 1989b. The multicultural seminary: Need for kenosis. *The Priest* (January): 35-39.

_____. 1989c. The pastoral plan, window of opportunity. *Origins* 19, no. 12 (August 17): 198-201.

_____. 1990a. The Hispanic presence: A moment of grace. *The Critic* 45, no. 1 (Fall): 48-59.

_____. 1990b. Hispanic theologians and the United States Catholic church. *New Theology Review* 3, no. 4 (November): 22-27.

_____. 1990c. The spirituality of the United States Hispanics: An introductory essay. *U.S. Catholic Historian* 9, no. 1 & 2 (Winter): 137-146.

_____. 1991. Amen! *Church* (Spring): 64.

_____. 1993. La Raza Cósmica: Rediscovering the Hispanic soul. *The Critic* (Spring): 46-53.

_____. 1994. "The challenge of evangelical/Pentecostal Christianity to Hispanic Catholicism." In *Hispanic Catholic culture in the U.S.: Issues and concerns,* edited by Jay P. Dolan and Allan Figueroa Deck, 409-439. Notre Dame, IN: University of Notre Dame Press.

Figueroa Deck, Allan, S.J., ed. 1992. *Frontiers of Hispanic theology in the U.S.* Maryknoll, NY: Orbis Books.

Fitzpatrick, Joseph P., S.J. 1984. The Latin American church in the United States. *Thought* 59, no. 233 (June): 244-254.

_____. 1985. Television, Hispanics and the Church. *America* 152, no. 11 (March 23): 232-234.

_____. 1988. The Hispanic poor in the American Catholic middle-class church. *Thought* 63 (June): 189-200.

Flores, Patricio. 1976. "Pastoral para los hispano-parlantes en los Estados Unidos." In *El Quetzal emplumece,* compiled by Carmela Montalvo and Leonardo Anguiano, 352-361. San Antonio, TX: Mexican American Cultural Center.

_____. 1978. The Catholic Hispanic servicemen. *La Luz* 7, no. 10 (October): 43.

_____. 1979. More leaders needed for Hispanic community. *La Luz* 8, no. 7 (August-September): 32.

_____. 1980a. "The Church: Diocesan and National." In *Prophets denied honor,* edited by Antonio M. Stevens-Arroyo, 187-195. Maryknoll, NY: Orbis Books.

_____. 1980b. "The Church must liberate." In *Prophets denied honor,* edited by Antonio M. Stevens-Arroyo, 220-225. Maryknoll, NY: Orbis Books.

Flores, Richard R. 1991. Chicanos, culture, and the borderlands: Reflections on worship. *Modern Liturgy* 18, no. 9: 16-17.

Flores, Richard R., ed. 1982. *Tomen y coman*. Miami, FL: Instituto de Liturgia Hispana.

Folliard, Dorothy. 1988. "Theological literature of the U.S.A. minorities." In *Convergences and differences,* edited by L. Boff and V. Elizondo, 90-95. Edinburgh, Scotland: T & T Clark.

_____. 1989. Sparks from the south: The growing impact of liberation theology on the United States Hispanic church. *International Review of Mission* 78 (April): 150-154.

Fontanez, Luis. 1980. "The theology of social justice." In *Prophets denied honor,* edited by Antonio M. Stevens-Arroyo, 233-236. Maryknoll, NY: Orbis Books.

Fukuyama, Francis. 1993. Immigrants and family values. *Commentary* 95 (May): 26-32.

Galilea, Segundo. 1981. *Religiosidad popular y pastoral hispano-americana*. New York: Centro Católico de Pastoral para Hispanos del Nordeste.

Galván, Elías. 1992. Hispanics: challenge and opportunity [United Methodist Church Hispanic ministry]. *Apuntes* 12 (Summer): 89-97.

García, Sixto J. 1993. Trinitarian theology. *Proceedings of the Catholic Theological Association* 48: 137-142.

Garcia-Treto, Francisco O. 1981. Historical perspectives on Hispanic missions. *Perkins Journal* 35 (Fall): 63-72.

Garcia-Treto, Francisco O., and R. Douglas Brackenridge. 1991. "Hispanic Presbyterians: Life in two cultures." In *The diversity of discipleship,* edited by M. Coalter, et al, 257-279. Louisville, KY: Westminster/John Knox Press.

Gastón, María Luisa. 1987. "Leadership development in the Hispanic community." In *Faith and culture: A multicultural catechetical resource,* edited by A. Peláez, 33-44. Washington, D.C.: Department of Education, United States Catholic Conference.

Gohr, Glenn. 1989. A dedicated ministry among Hispanics: Demetrio and Nellie Bazan. *Assemblies of God Heritage* 9 (Fall): 7-9, 17.

Goizueta, Roberto. 1991. "The church and Hispanics in the United States: From empowerment to solidarity." In *Theologies of empowerment,* edited by Michael Downey, 160- 175. New York: Crossroads.

_____. 1992a. "United States Hispanic theology and the challenge of pluralism." In *Frontiers of Hispanic theology in the United States,* edited by Allan Figueroa Deck, 1-22. New York: Orbis Books.

_____. 1992b. Nosotros: Toward a U.S. Hispanic anthropology. *Listening* 27, no. 1 (Winter): 55-69.

Goizueta, Roberto, ed. 1992. *We are a people: Initiatives in Hispanic American theology*. Minneapolis, MN: Fortress Press.

Gómez, Roberto L. 1982. Pastoral care and counseling in a Mexican American setting. *Apuntes: Reflexiones Teológicas desde el Margen Hispano* 2, no. 2 (Summer): 31-39.

González, Justo L. 1981a. Prophets in the king's sanctuary. *Apuntes: Reflexiones Teológicas desde el Margen Hispano* 1, no. 1: 3-6.

_____. 1981b. Towards a new reading of history. *Apuntes: Reflexiones Teológicas desde el Margen Hispano* 1 (Fall): 4- 14.

_____. 1987. Hacia un redescubrimiento de nuestra misión. *Apuntes: Reflexiones Teológicas desde el Margen Hispano* 7 (Fall): 51-60.

_____. 1990a. *Mañana: Christian theology from a Hispanic perspective*. Nashville: Abingdon Press.

_____. 1990b. The next ten years [of Apuntes and Hispanic theology]. *Apuntes* 10 (Winter): 84-94.

González, Justo L., ed. 1991. *Each in our own tongue: A history of Hispanic United Methodism*. Nashville, TN: Abingdon Press.

_____. 1992a. *Voces: Voices from the Hispanic church*. Nashville, TN: Abingdon Press.

_____. 1992b. Redescubrimiento: 500 years of Hispanic Christianity, 1492-1992. *Apuntes* 12 (Summer): 35-107.

Granjon, Henry. 1986. *Along the Rio Grande: A pastoral visit to southwest New Mexico in 1902*. Albuquerque, NM: The Historical Society of New Mexico and University of New Mexico Press.

Guerrero, Andrés G. 1983. *Church and peace*. Edinburgh, Scotland: T & T Clark.

_____. 1984. *Transmission of the faith in the USA*. Edinburgh, Scotland: T & T Clark.

_____. 1987. *A Chicano theology*. New York: Orbis Books.

Hall, Suzanne. 1986. The Hispanic presence: Implications for Catholic educators. *Momentum* 17, no. 1 (February): 43-45.

Hammond, John. 1985. Arroz. *Modern Liturgy* 12, no. 2 (March): 14.

Hanlon, Don. 1991. The confrontation of two dissimilar cultures: The adobe church in New Mexico. *Journal of the Interfaith Forum on Religion, Art, and Architecture* (Winter): 17-20.

Haselden, Kyle. 1964. *Death of a myth*. New York: Friendship Press.

Hatch, James D. 1989. Juan and James: Pointers toward solutions? *Presbyterion: A Journal for the Eldership-Covenant Seminary Review* 15 (Fall): 39-47.

Hay, Stephen. 1990. A pastoral response to amnesty applicants in a West Texas diocese. *Migration World Magazine* 18, no. 3-4: 30-33.

Hemrick, Eugene, ed. 1993. *Strangers and aliens no longer.* Part One: The Hispanic Presence in the Church in the United States. Washington, D.C.: NCCB/USCC.

Hernández, Edwin. 1992. *Jesús,* the mestizo. *Insight* (January). [Special Hispanic Issue.]

_____. Forthcoming. "Hung between two worlds: Towards a Hispanic youth ministry." In *Youth ministry today,* edited by Bailey Gillespie. Riverside, CA: La Sierra University Press.

Hernández, Lydia. 1986. La mujer chicana y la justicia económica. *Apuntes: Reflexiones Teológicas desde el Margen Hispano* 6 (Winter): 81-83.

Herrera, Marina. 1978. Hispanics in the church: Issues and visions. *Military Chaplains' Review* (Fall).

_____. 1979a. What is multicultural catechesis. *Dimensions* (March).

_____. 1979b. A Hispanic catechetical project. *Dimensions* (April).

_____. 1979c. Proclaiming a fascinating god. *Dimensions* (Summer).

_____. 1979d. The Hispanic challenge. *Religious Education* 74, no. 5 (September-October).

_____. 1979e. *Methodology and themes for Hispanic catechesis.* Washington D.C.: Department of Education of the United States Catholic Conference.

_____. 1980a. Pastoral care in a multicultural society. *Camillian, Journal of the National Association of Catholic Chaplains* 19, no. 1 (Spring).

_____. 1980b. Catechetics for a multicultural society. *Catechist* (April).

_____. 1980c. Catechetical institutes for lay Hispanics. *Dimensions* (May-June).

_____. 1980d. The religious education of Hispanics in a multicultural church. *New Catholic World* (July-August).

_____. 1980e. Hispanics' cultural riches and parish renewal. *Parish.*

_____. 1981. Popular piety as a parish resource. *Service* no. 3.

_____. 1982a. Hispanics: How can the church respond to their presence? *PACE* 12 (April-May).

_____. 1982b. Sharing scripture with the non-print oriented. *Liturgy* 2, no. 3.

_____. 1982c. *Hablemos del compadrazgo en la familia hispana.* Chicago: Claretian Publications.

_____. 1983a. "Multicultural adult catechesis: What is it and for whom?" In *Christian adulthood: A catechetical resource.* Washington, D.C.: United States Catholic Conference.

_____. 1983b. Mary in Hispanic piety. *Catechist* (April): 18.

_____. 1984. *Adult religious education for the Hispanic community.* The National Conference of Diocesan Directors of Religious Education.

_____. 1985a. Religion and culture in the Hispanic community as a context for religious education: Impact of popular religiosity on U.S. Hispanics. *The Living Light* 21, no. 2 (January).

_____. 1985b. *LASER: Creating unity in diversity.* The National Conference for Interracial Justice.

_____. 1985c. Popular religiosity and liturgical education. *Liturgy* 5, no. 1.

_____. 1986. First communion celebration in Hispanic practice. *Catechist* (February): 14-15.

_____. 1987. "Theoretical foundations for multicultural catechesis." In *Faith and culture: A multicultural catechetical resource,* edited by A. Pelaez. Washington, D.C.: Department of Education, USCC.

_____. 1989. Providence and histories: One Hispanic's view. *The Catholic Theology Society of America, Proceedings of the Forty-Fourth Annual Convention* 44: 7-11.

_____. 1994. "The context and development of Hispanic ecclesial leadership." In *Hispanic Catholic culture in the U.S.: Issues and concerns,* edited by Jay P. Dolan and Allan Figueroa Deck, 166-205. Notre Dame, IN: University of Notre Dame Press.

Herrera, Marina, and Jaime R. Vidal. 1990. Evangelization: Then and now. *New Theology Review* (November): 6-21.

Herrera, Marina, Thea Bowman, Martin J. Carter, and Jaime R. Vidal. 1988. *Pentecost: A feast for all peoples, celebrating the multicultural/multiracial church.* National Catholic Conference for Interracial Justice.

Hinojosa, Juan-Lorenzo. 1991. Formation in Hispanic ministry. *Review for Religious* 50, no. 5 (September/October): 722-729.

_____. 1992. "Culture, spirituality, and U.S. Hispanics." In *Frontiers of Hispanic theology in the United States,* edited by A. Figueroa Deck, 154-164. Maryknoll, NY: Orbis Books.

Hoehn, Richard A. 1976. Chicano ethos: An Anglo view. *Lutheran Quarterly* 28 (May): 166-172.

_____. 1988. A guide to Hispanic-American culture in south Texas. *Apuntes: Reflexiones Teológicas desde el Margen Hispano* 8 (Winter): 83-87.

Hoffman, Pat. 1987. *Ministry of the dispossessed: Learning from the farm worker movement.* Los Angeles, CA: Wallace Press.

Holland, Clifton L. 1974. *The religious expression of Hispanic Los Angeles: A Protestant case study.* Pasadena: William Carey Library.

_____. 1975. Anglo-Hispanic Protestant tensions in southern California. *Missiology: An International Review* 3 (July): 323-345.

Hughes, Cornelius G. 1992. Views from the pews: Hispanic and Anglo Catholics in a changing church [impact of US priest shortage]. *Review of Religious Research* 33 (June): 364-75.

Huitrado-Hizo, Juan José. 1990. Hispanic popular religiosity: The expression of a people coming to life. *New Theology Review* 3, no. 4 (November): 43-55.

Icaza, Rosa María. 1989. Spirituality of the Mexican American people. *Worship* 63, no. 3 (May): 232-246.

Inda, Caridad. 1985. "New priorities, new potential." In *Midwives of the future,* edited by A. Ware, 111-116.

Isasi-Díaz, Ada María. 1979. Silent women will never be heard. *Missiology* 7, no. 3 (July): 295-301.

_____. 1980. "The people of God on the move—chronicle of a history." In *Prophets denied honor,* edited by Antonio M. Stevens-Arroyo, 330-333. Maryknoll, NY: Orbis Books.

_____. 1982. La mujer hispana: Voz profética en la iglesia de los Estados Unidos. *Informes de Pro Mundi Vita América Latina* 28: 1-27.

_____. 1983. "A liberationist perspective on peace and social justice." In *Education for peace and justice,* edited by Padraic O'Hare, 223-233. San Francisco: Harper & Row.

_____. 1985. "Toward an understanding of feminismo hispano in the USA." In *Women's consciousness, women's conscience,* edited by Barbara Hilkert Andolsen, Christina Gudorf, and Mary D. Pellauer, 51-61. Houston, TX: Winston Press.

_____. 1986. Apuntes for a Hispanic women's theology of liberation. *Apuntes* [Dallas] (Fall): 61-71.

_____. 1988. "A Hispanic garden in a foreign land." In *Inheriting our mothers' garden,* edited by Ada María Isasi- Díaz, et al. Louisville, KY: Westminster Press.

_____. 1989a. "Mujeristas: A name of our own." In *The future of liberation theology,* edited by Marc H. Ellis and Otto Maduro, 410-419. Maryknoll, NY: Orbis Books.

_____. 1989b. A platform for original voices. *Christianity and Crisis* 49, no. 9 (12 June): 191-192.

_____. 1990a. "Solidarity: Love of neighbor in the 1980's." In *Lift every voice: Constructing Christian theologies from the underside,* edited by Susan Brooks Thistlethwaite and Mary Potter Engel, 31-40. San Francisco: Harper & Row.

_____. 1990b. "The Bible and mujerista theology." In *Lift every voice: Constructing Christian theologies from the underside,* edited by Susan Brooks Thistlethwaite and Mary Potter Engel, 261-269. San Francisco: Harper & Row.

_____. 1991a. Hispanics in America: Starting points. *Christianity and Crisis: A Christian Journal of Opinion* 51 (May 13): 150-152.

_____. 1991b. "Hispanic women in the Roman Catholic Church." In *Women and church: The challenge of Ecumenical solidarity in an age of alienation,* edited by Melanie A. May, 13-17. Grand Rapids, MI: W.B. Eerdmans.

_____. 1992. Mujerista theology's method: A liberative praxis, a way of life. *Listening* 27, no. 1 (Winter): 41-54.

_____. 1993a. *En la lucha—in the struggle: A Hispanic women's liberation theology.* Minneapolis, MN: Fortress Press.

_____. 1993b. Defining our proyecto histórico: Mujerista strategies for liberation. *The Journal of Feminist Studies in Religion* 9, no. 1-2 (Spring/Fall): 17-28.

_____. 1994. La vida de las mujeres hispanas. *Cristianismo y Sociedad* [Guayaquil, Ecuador] 31-32, no. 118-119: 43-62.

Isasi-Díaz, Ada María, and Yolanda Tarango. 1988. *Hispanic women, prophetic voice in the church: Toward a Hispanic women's liberation theology.* San Francisco: Harper and Row.

Isasi-Díaz, Ada María, et al. 1985. *The Mudflower collective.* Cleveland, OH: Pilgrim Press.

_____. 1992. Mujeristas: who we are and what we are about [roundtable discussion]. *Journal of Feminist Studies in Religion* 8 (Spring): 105-25.

Jaramillo, Luis. 1971. A modern parable; too late your tears!! *El Cuaderno* 1, no. 1: 15-17.

Jensen, Carol L. 1987. "Deserts, diversity, and self- determination: A history of the Catholic parish in the intermountain west." In *The American Catholic parish,* Vol. 2, edited by Jay P. Dolan, 137-276. New York: Paulist Press.

Jiménez, Pablo A., ed. 1994. *Lumbrera a nuestro camino.* Miami, FL: Editorial Caribe.

Jiménez, Rodolfo. 1991. *Misión de Jesús,* McFarland, California, and Alfa y Omega, Lancaster, Pennsylvania [Church of the Brethren new church cases histories]. *Brethren Life and Thought* 36 (Summer): 199-202.

Jones, Donald L. 1993. Social justice education and the Hispanic experience. *Proceedings of the Catholic Theological Association* 48: 130.

Juárez, José Roberto. 1973. La iglesia católica y el chicano en sud Texas, 1836-1911. *Aztlan* 4, no. 2 (Fall): 217-255.

Juárez-Palma, Nils. 1992. Pastoral care to Hispanic military families. *Military Chaplains' Review* (Summer): 9-18.

Kinney, Bruce, D.D. 1918. "Problem three: The Spanish in America." In *Frontier Missionary Problems,* 97-117. New York: F. Revell Co.

Krass, Alfred C. 1980. Strikers and Ohio churches: In the soup. *The Christian Century* 97 (August 13-20): 796-798.

Lara-Braud, Jorge. 1992. "Reflexiones teológicas sobre la migración." In *Voces: Voices from the Hispanic church,* edited by Justo González, 87-91. Nashville, TN: Abingdon.

LeBerthon, Ted. 1957. The church and the bracero. *The Catholic Worker* 24, 2 (September).

Lloyd-Sidle, Patricia J., ed. 1989. Called to the border: A paradigm for mission. *International Review of Mission* 78 (April): 135-220.

Loperena, William. 1980a. "Episcopitis." In *Prophets denied honor,* edited by Antonio M. Stevens-Arroyo, 243-245. Maryknoll, NY: Orbis Books.

_____. 1980b. "The phenomenon of migration as a central religious experience." In *Prophets denied honor,* edited by Antonio M. Stevens-Arroyo, 262-268. Maryknoll, NY: Orbis Books.

López, Carlos A. 1987. Hymn singing in the Hispanic tradition. *Reformed Liturgy and Music* 21 (Summer): 156-157.

López, Hugo L. 1982. Toward a theology of migration. *Apuntes: Reflexiones Teológicas desde el Margen Hispano* 2, no. 3 (Fall): 68-71.

Loya, Gloria Inés. 1992. "The Hispanic woman: pasionaria and pastora of the Hispanic community." In *Frontiers of Hispanic theology,* edited by Allan F. Deck, 124-133. Maryknoll, NY: Orbis Books.

Lucas, Isidro. 1981. *The browning of America: The Hispanic revolution in the American church.* Chicago: Fides\ Claretian.

Lucey, Robert E. 1947. Christianizing Mexican Catholics. *America* 77 (August): 541.

Luna, David. 1986. Patterns of faith: Woven together in life and mission. *American Baptist Quarterly* 5, no. 4 (December): 393-397.

Luna, Roger B. 1980. "Why so few Mexican-American priests?" In *Prophets denied honor,* edited by Antonio M. Stevens-Arroyo, 160-163. Maryknoll, NY: Orbis Books.

Machado, Federico J. 1991. Iglesia el Siervo del Señor: Retaining old Catholic traditions in a new Reformed church. *Reformed Worship* 19 (March): 7-9.

Malspina, Ann. 1989. Serving society and church. *Vista* 4, no. 29 (March): 10.

Marrero, Gilberto. 1972. Hispanic American and liberation. *Church and Society* (January/February): 25-34.

Martínez, Dolorita. 1990. Basic Christian communities: A new model of church within the United States Hispanic community. *New Theology Review* 3, no. 4 (November): 35-42.

Martínez, Jill. 1986. Worship and the search for community in the Presbyterian church (USA): The Hispanic experience. *Church and Society* 76, no. 4 (March-April): 42-46.

————. 1989. In search of an inclusive community. *Apuntes: Reflexiones Teológicas desde el Margen Hispano* 9 (Spring): 3-9.

Martínez, Juan. 1987. Hispanics in California: Myth and opportunity. *Direction: A Quarterly Publication of Mennonite Brethren Schools* 16 (Spring): 47-56.

Martínez, Germán, O.S.B. 1993. "Hispanic American spirituality." In *The new dictionary of Catholic spirituality,* edited by Michael Downey, 473-476. Collegeville, MN: The Liturgical Press.

Massa, Mark S. 1991. "Disciples in a mission land: The Christian church in New York City." In *A case study of mainstream Protestantism,* edited by D. Williams, 469-490. Grand Rapids, MI: W. B. Eedermans Publishing Co.

Matovina, Timothy. 1989. Liturgy, popular rites, and popular spirituality. *Worship* 63 (July): 351-361.

_____. 1991a. Liturgy and popular expressions of faith: A look at the works of Virgil Elizondo. *Worship* 63, no. 5 (September): 436-444.

_____. 1991b. The Italian 'problem' and the Hispanic opportunity. *America* 165, no. 15 (November 16): 362-363.

_____. 1993. Ministries and the servant community. *Worship* 67, no. 4 (July): 351-360.

Maur (St.) Theological Center [Indianapolis]. 1980. [Entire issue on Hispanics] *The City of God Journal* 2, no. 2 (Fall).

McConnell, Taylor. 1984. Cross-cultural ministries with families. *Religious Education* 79 (Summer): 353-366.

McConnell, Taylor, and June McConnell. 1991. Cross-cultural ministry with church and family: The final report of a research project. *Religious Education* 86 (Fall): 581-596.

Méndez de Guzmán, Noelle. 1989. *La verdadera historia: Aparición de la Virgen del Rosario.* Puerto Rico.

Mikell, Gwendolyn. 1990. "Catholic diversity, pluralism, and interracial/intercultural education." In *Georgetown at two hundred,* edited by W. McFadden, 213-236. Washington, D.C.: Georgetown University Press.

Miranda, Jesse. 1989. Realizing the Hispanic dream. *Christianity Today* 33 (March 3): 37-40.

Muñiz-Rocha, William. 1988. Sí hay judíos y griegos, esclavos y libres. *Apuntes: Reflexiones Teológicas desde el Margen Hispano* 8 (Winter): 88-91.

Murphy, Joseph M. 1979. Traces of African religiosity came to U.S. as Santería. *Liturgy* (November-December): 10-12.

_____. 1988. *Santería: An African religion in America.* Boston: Beacon Press.

Nagy, Alex. 1979. Presbyters and Chicanos: Toward full partnership in liberation. *Sylloge Excerptorum* 49: 35-50.

Náñez, Alfredo. 1978. Transition from Anglo to Mexican American leadership in the Rio Grande conference. *Methodist History* 16 (January): 67-74.

National pastoral plan for Hispanic ministry. 1988. *Migration World Magazine* 16, no. 2: 34-35.

Navarro, Armando. 1980. The development of a new concept. *Agenda* 10, 5 (September/October).

New Catholic World. 1980. *New Catholic World* (July/August). [Entire Issue Devoted to Hispanic Catholics.]

Nichols, David. 1992. "Virgil Elizondo: A particular man [rector, San Fernando Cathedral, San Antonio; biog sketch]" In *Sources of inspiration,* edited by G. Maeroff, 86-107. Kansas City, MO: Sheed & Ward.

Nieto, Leo. 1975. The Chicano movement and the churches in the United States. *Perkins Journal of Theology* 29 (Fall): 32- 41.

Orozco, E. C. 1980. Republican Protestantism in Aztlan: The encounter between Mexicanism and Anglo-Saxon secular humanism in the United States Southwest. [Glandale, C.A.]: The Petereins Press.

Ortiz, José L., ed. 1989. Grow by caring among Hispanic congregations in the United States and Puerto Rico. *American Baptist Quarterly* 8 (September): 202-212.

Ortiz, Manuel. 1988. The rise of Spiritism in North America. *Urban Mission* 5 (March): 11-17.

Pachuco Cultures Research and Development. 1980. *Gospel of the wicked cross: The gospel according to the Pachuco.* Los Angeles, CA: Pachuco Press.

Pagán, Samuel. 1991. Education, mission, and Hispanics: Implications for church renewal. *Lexington Theological Quarterly* 26 (July-October):93-100.

Parrilla Bonilla, Antulio, SJ. 1971. *Puerto Rico: Supervivencia y liberacíon.* Río Piedras, PR: Ediciones Librería Internacional.

_____. 1980a. "The role of Christians in Puerto Rico." In *Prophets denied honor,* edited by Antonio M. Stevens-Arroyo, 91-93. Maryknoll, NY: Orbis Books.

_____. 1980b. "The reality of the present North American society." In *Prophets denied honor,* edited by Antonio M. Stevens-Arroyo, 93-94. Maryknoll, NY: Orbis Books.

_____. 1990. *Estampas Monserratinas: Unas Crónicas y Tres Cuentos.* Hormigüeros, PR: Editorial Cuarto Siglo.

Pazmino, Robert W. 1988. Double dutch: Reflections of an Hispanic North-American on multicultural religious education. *Apuntes: Reflexiones Teológicas desde el Margen Hispano* 8 (Summer): 27-37.

Peña, Roberto. 1980. "Concerning multi-Hispanic urban solidarity." In *Prophets denied honor,* edited by Antonio M. Stevens-Arroyo, 286-288. Maryknoll, NY: Orbis Books.

Pérez, Arturo J. 1981. Baptism in the Hispanic community. *Emmanuel Magazine* 87, no. 2 (February): 77-86.

_____. 1983. Lent: Conversion liturgy. *Hosana* 1, no. 1 (Spring).

_____. 1988. *Popular Catholicism: A Hispanic perspective.* Washington D.C.: The Pastoral Press.

_____. 1990. Signs of the times: Toward a Hispanic rite, 'quizás'. *New Theology Review* 3, no. 4 (November): 80-88.

_____. 1994. "The history of Hispanic liturgy since 1965." In *Hispanic Catholic culture in the U.S.: Issues and concerns,* edited by Jay P. Dolan and Allan Figueroa Deck, 360-408. Notre Dame, IN: University of Notre Dame Press.

Pérez y González, María E. 1994. *Spiritual fast: To strengthen community among women of all cultures.* Chicago, IL: Evangelical Lutheran Church in America, Commission for Women.

Pineda, Ana María. 1988. Hispanic identity. *Church Magazine* (Winter): 51-55.

_____. 1989. The Hispanic presence: Hope and challenge for catholicity. *New Theology Review* 2, no. 3 (August): 30-36.

_____. 1990. Pastoral de conjunto. *New Theology Review* 3, no. 4: 28-34.

Pinto Alicea, Inés. 1990. Catholic leaders concerned over limits in migrant health care. *Migration World Magazine* 18, no. 2: 25.

Piña, Roberto, Yolanda Tarango, and Timothy Matovina. 1993. U.S. Hispanic and Latin American theologies: Critical distinctions. *Proceedings of the Catholic Theological Association of America* 48: 128-130.

Ponce, Frank. Rev. 1980. The enculturation of Hispanics in the Catholic church. *Agenda* 10, no. 6 (November-December): 11-15.

_____. 1981. Spanish speaking Catholics in the United States. *Pro Mundi Vita: Dossier* (January 12).

_____. 1982. "Hispanic community." In *Tomorrow's church,* edited by E. Herr, 164-192. Chicago, IL: Thomas More Press.

Pope-Levison, Priscilla. 1988. Comprehensive and contextual: The evangelism of Orlando Costas. *Journal of the Academy for Evangelism in Theological Education* 4: 4-14.

Power, David. 1993. Hispanic pastoral theology. *Proceedings of the Catholic Theological Association of America* 48: 126-127.

Privett, Stephen A. 1988. *The U.S. Catholic church and its Hispanic members: The pastoral vision of Archbishop Robert E. Lucey.* San Antonio, TX: Trinity University Press.

Quevedo, Eduardo. 1968. The Catholic church in America. *Con Safos* 1, no. 2 (Fall): 11.

Quezada Agostini, Milagros. 1990. With güiros and maracas: Hispanic Christian music in a charismatic church. *Hymn* 41 (April): 30-33.

Quiñones-Ortiz, Javier. 1991. The Mestizo journey: Challenges for Hispanic theology. *Apuntes: Reflexiones Teológicas desde el Margen Hispano* 11 (Fall): 62-72.

_____. 1993. Psalm 72: On confronting rulers in urban society. *Apuntes: Reflexiones Teológicas desde el Margen Hispano* 13 (Fall): 180-189.

Ramírez, Ricardo. 1977. Liturgy from the Mexican-American perspective. *Worship* 57 (July): 293.

_____. 1978. La familia: Channel of faith and culture. *La Luz* 7 no. 10 (October): 20-22.

_____. 1983. Reflections on the hispanicization of the liturgy. *Worship* 57 (January): 26-34.

_____. 1986. *El descubrimiento del tesoro más rico en la liturgia: El rito de la iniciación cristiana para adultos.* Miami, Fl.: Instituto de Liturgia Hispana.

_____. 1992. The challenge of ecumenism to Hispanic Christians. *Ecumenical Trends* 21: 117,128-131.

Recinos, Harold. 1989. Walking with Christ in the barrio. *The Other Side* 25 (March-April): 30-32.

_____. 1992. "Militarism and the poor." In *Voces: Voices from the Hispanic church,* edited by Justo González, 159-165. Nashville, TN: Avingdon.

Report on ministry to migrant workers. 1975. *La Luz* 4, no. 3 (June): 6.

Reyes, Abraham. 1972. Autochthonous church and liberation. *El Cuaderno* 2, no. 1: 14-15.

Riebe-Estrella, Gary. 1990. Underneath Hispanic vocations. *New Theology Review* 3, no. 4 (November): 72-79.

_____. 1992. The challenge of ministerial formation [US Latinos]. *Missiology* 20 (April): 269-74.

Rips, Geoffrey. 1988. A new spirit flows along the Rio Grande. *In These Times* 12, no. 25 (May 18): 12-13, 22.

Rivas, Yolanda E. 1982. Confrontación y reconciliación. *Apuntes: Reflexiones Teológicas desde el Margen Hispano* 2, no. 2 (Summer): 40-47.

Rivera, Orlando. 1978. "Mormonism and the Chicano." In *Mormonism: A faith for all cultures,* edited by F. LaMond Tullis, 115-126. Provo, Utah: Brigham Young University Press.

Rivera-Pagán, Luis N. 1989. *Senderos teológicos: El pensamiento evangélico puertorriqueño.* Río Piedras, PR: Editorial La Reforma.

————. 1992. *A violent evangelism: The political and religious conquest of the Americas.* Louisville, KY: Westminster-John Knox Press.

Rivera, Raymond. 1980. "The political and social ramifications of indigenous Pentecostalism." In *Prophets denied honor,* edited by Antonio M. Stevens-Arroyo, 339-341. Maryknoll, NY: Orbis Books.

Rodríguez, Edmundo. 1976. "The invisible nation: The poor Mexican-Americans of the Southwest." In *El Quetzal emplumece,* compiled by Carmela Montalvo and Leonardo Anguiano, 371-380. San Antonio, TX: Mexican American Cultural Center.

————. 1980. "Parish catechetics." In *Prophets denied honor,* edited by Antonio M. Stevens-Arroyo, 226-229. Maryknoll, NY: Orbis Books.

————. 1994. "The Hispanic community and church movements: Schools of leadership." In *Hispanic Catholic culture in the U.S.: Issues and concerns,* edited by Jay P. Dolan and Allan Figueroa Deck, 206-239. Notre Dame, IN: University of Notre Dame Press.

Rodríguez, José A. 1990. Hispanic hymns in the new hymnal. *Reformed Liturgy and Music* 24 (Spring): 82-83.

Rodríguez, José David. 1990. De "apuntes" a "esbozo": diez años de reflexión [Hispanic-American theology]. *Apuntes: Reflexiones Teológicas desde el Margen Hispano* 10 (Winter): 75-83.

————. 1991. The challenge of Hispanic ministry (reflections on John 4). *Currents in Theology and Mission* 18 (December): 420-26.

Rodríguez Díaz, Daniel R., and David Cortés Fuentes, eds. 1994. *Hidden stories: Unveiling the history of the Latino church.* Decatur, GA: AETH.

Romero, C. Gilbert. 1979. Teología de las raices de un pueblo: Los penitentes de Nuevo México. *Servir* (Mexico) 15: 609- 630.

_____. 1981. On choosing a symbol system for a Hispanic theology. *Apuntes: Reflexiones Teológicas desde el Margen Hispano* 1, no. 4: 16-20.

_____. 1985. Self-affirmation of the Hispanic church. *The Ecumenist* 23, no. 3 (March-April): 39-42.

_____. 1991. *Hispanic devotional piety: Tracing the biblical roots.* Maryknoll, New York: Orbis Books.

_____. 1993. The Bible, revelation and Marian devotion. *Marian Studies* 44.

Rosado, Caleb. 1989a. The church, the city, and the compassionate Christ. *Apuntes: Reflexiones Teológicas desde el Margen Hispano* 9 (Summer): 27-35. Reprinted, 1992, in *Voces: Voices from the Hispanic church,* edited by Justo L. González. Nashville, TN: Abingdon Press.

_____. 1989b. Thoughts on a Puerto Rican theology of community. *Apuntes: Reflexiones Teológicas desde el Margen Hispano* 9 (Spring): 10-12.

_____. 1990. In search of identity. *El Sentinela* (September).

_____. 1992. The Christian response to the L.A. riots. *Adventist Review* (June 18).

_____. 1994. El papel de la teología de la liberación en la identidad social de los latinos. *Cristianismo y Sociedad* [Guayaquil, Ecuador] 31-32, no. 118-119: 63-78.

Rosas, Carlos. 1977. Mexican Americans sing because they feel like singing. *Pastoral Music* 1, no. 5 (June-July): 14-17.

Ross, Susan. 1993. Sexual ethics: Women in the Latino community. *Proceedings of the Catholic Theological Association of America* 48: 118-119.

Rossing, John P. 1988. Mestizaje and marginality: A Hispanic American theology. *Theology Today* 45 (October): 293-304.

Ruiz, Jean-Pierre. 1994. Beginning to read the Bible in Spanish: An initial assessment. *Journal of Hispanic-Latino Theology* 1, no. 2 (February): 28-50.

Saldigloria, Romeo F. 1980. "Religious problems of the Hispanos in the city of New York." In *Prophets denied honor,* edited by Antonio M. Stevens-Arroyo, 166-169. Maryknoll, NY: Orbis Books.

Salinas, Rodolfo. 1970. The consistent inconsistency of the church. *Con Safos* 2, no. 35: 37.

Salomón, Esaul. 1991. The role of liturgy in Hispanic Lutheran churches. *Lutheran Forum* 25 (May): 30-31.

Sánchez, Jorge E. 1989. La educación bíblica en nuestra iglesia hispana. *Apuntes: Reflexiones Teológicas desde el Margen Hispano* 9 (Summer): 35-38.

Santillán Baert, María Luisa. 1992. "The Church and liberation." In *Voces: Voices from the Hispanic church,* edited by Justo González, 68-71. Nashville, TN: Abingdon.

Schreiter, Robert. 1993. Theology and culture from a Caribbean perspective. *Proceedings of the Catholic Theological Association of America* 48: 103-104.

Segovia, Fernando F. 1991. A new manifest destiny: The emerging theological voice of Hispanic Americans. *Religious Studies Review* 17 (April): 102-109.

_____. 1992. Two places and no place on which to stand: Mixture and otherness in Hispanic American theology. *Listening* 27, no. 1 (Winter): 26-40.

Segovia, Fernando F., ed. 1992. Hispanic Americans in theology and the church. *Listening* 27 (Winter): 3-84.

Solivan, Samuel. 1990. Orthopathos: Interlocutor between orthodoxy and praxis. *Andover Newton Review* 1 (Winter): 19-25.

Sosa, Juan J. 1976. "Santa Bárbara y San Lázaro." In *Cuba: Diaspora,* 101-103. Miami, FL: Christian Commitment Foundation.

_____. 1979. An Anglo-Hispanic dilemma: Liturgical piety or popular piety. *Liturgy* 24, no. 6 (November-December): 7-9.

_____. 1980. "Popular piety: An integral element of the conversion process." In *Christian initiation resources,* Vol. 1, 249-254. New York: Sadlier.

_____. 1981a. Liturgy in two languages…Some principles. *Pastoral Music* 5, no. 6 (August-September): 36-38.

_____. 1981b. El ministerio de la música litúrgica en nuestras comunidades hispanas. *Liturgy* 80: 10-11. [Chicago: Office for Divine Worship]

_____. 1982. Illness and healing in Hispanic communities. *Liturgy* 2: 62-67.

_____. 1983a. Let us pray…en español. *Liturgy* 3, no. 2 (Spring): 63-67.

_____. 1983b. Liturgy in three languages. *Pastoral Music* 7, no. 3 (February-March): 13-15.

_____. 1989. Texto Único: A unified liturgical text for Spanish speaking Catholics. *Liturgy* 80 (May-June): 9-10.

_____. 1992a. "Reflections from the Hispanic viewpoint [post-Vatican II liturgies]." In *The awakening church,* edited by L. J. Madden, 121-24. Collegeville, MN: Liturgical Press.

_____. 1992b. Liturgia, religiosidad popular y evangelización: El ejemplo de la liturgia hispana en los Estados Unidos. *Phase* 32, no. 190 (July-August): 295-304.

Soto, Antonio. 1970. Migrants in your parish. *The Homiletic and Pastoral Review,* 887-897.

_____. 1979. The church in California and the Chicano: A sociological analysis. *Grito del Sol* 4, no. 1: 47-74.

Soto, Juan Sigifredo. 1986. En torno a la transfiguración. *Apuntes: Reflexiones Teológicas desde el Margen Hispano* 6, no. 2 (Summer): 40-43.

Soto, Pedro Juan. 1987. "The Islander." In *Images and Identities,* edited by Asela Rodriguez de Laguna. Newark, NJ: Rutgers, The State University of New Jersey.

Soto, Rose Marie. 1989. 'Divine' choice. *Intercambios Femeniles* 3, no. 3 (Winter): 15.

Sotomayor-Chávez, Marta. 1982. Latin American migration. *Apuntes: Reflexiones Teológicas desde el Margen Hispano* 2 (Spring): 8-14.

_____. 1987. The future for Hispanics. *ESA: Engage/Social Action* 15 (March): 19-29.

Stacey, Gerald F., ed. 1982. From stranger to neighbor. *Church and Society* 72 (May-June): 1-71.

Stevens-Arroyo, Anthony M. 1967a. Culture, tomorrow's parish and the church today. *Ave María* 106, no. 8 (April 9): 16-18.

_____. 1967b. Some of your best friends are Puerto Ricans. *The Sign* 47, no. 4 (November): 22-27.

_____. 1975. Towards a definition of the theology of ethnicity. *Compassion* 4, no. 6: 1.

_____. 1976a. Toward an ethnic theology. *The New Catholic World* 119, no. 1311 (May-June): 139-142.

_____. 1976b. What is the ethnicity of the Catholic Church? *The Priest* 32, no. 11 (November): 37-41.

_____. 1976c. A Padre in Cuba. *PADRES Newsletter* 6, no. 3 (Fall): 24ff.

_____. 1976d. The American Catholic church faces ethnicity and migration. *Migration Today* 4, no. 5 (December):9ff.

_____. 1977. Marxism and the Hispanic movements of the United States. *New Catholic World* 220, no. 1317 (May-June): 126- 128.

_____. 1980. "Puerto Rican Struggles in the Catholic Church." In *The Puerto Rican struggle: Essays on survival in the United States,* edited by C. Rodríguez, V. Sánchez Korrol, and J.O. Alers, 129-139. Maplewood, NJ: Waterfront Press.

_____. 1981. "The Indian reality of Latin America's history." In *Seeds of a people's church: Challenge and promise from the underside of history,* edited by L. Unger and K. Schultz, 11-14. Detroit: Neil C. McMath Lectureship.

_____. 1987. Cahensly revisited? The national pastoral encounter of America's Hispanic Catholics. *Migration World* 15, no. 3: 16-19.

_____. Forthcoming. Praxis y persistencia de la religión Taína. *Anales del Caribe.* Habana, Cuba: Casa de las Américas.

_____. In press. "Jaime Balmes Redux: Catholicism as civilization in the political philosophy of Pedro Albizu Campos." In *Bridging the Atlantic: Iberian and Latin American thought in historical perspective,* edited by Marina Pérez de Mediola and Panivong Norindr. Albany: State University of New York Press.

Stevens-Arroyo, Anthony M., and Ana María Díaz Ramírez. 1980. The Hispano model of church: A people on the march. *New Catholic World* 223, no. 1336 (July-August): 153-157.

Stevens-Arroyo, Anthony M., and Virgilio Elizondo. 1975. "The Spanish-speaking." In *Liberty and justice for all,* edited by Bishops' Bicentennial Committee, 37-41. Washington, D.C.: USCC.

Sylvest, Edwin E., Jr. 1987. Rethinking the 'discovery' of the Americas: A provisional historico-theological reflection. *Apuntes: Reflexiones Teológicas desde el Margen Hispano* 7 (Spring): 3-13.

Tapia, Andrés. 1991. Viva los evangelicos! *Christianity Today* (October 28): 16-22.

Tarango, Yolanda. 1989. The church struggling to be universal: A Mexican American perspective. *International Review of Mission* 78 (April): 167-173.

_____. 1990. The Hispanic woman and her role in the church. *New Theology Review* 3, no. 4 (November): 56-61.

Teja, Gary, and Emily R. Brink. 1991. Alabaré a mi Señor—I will praise my Lord: A service in the Hispanic tradition. *Reformed Worship,* no. 21 (Summer): 30-31.

Toledo, Reinaldo. 1983. Cuban-American United Methodists: One part of the exile population. *Engage/Social Action* 11 (December): 36-38.

Tolson, Mike. 1985. Sanctuary movement attacked. *Texas Observer* 77, no. 1 (January): 4-5.

Torres, José. 1987. "The religion of machismo." In *Once a Catholic,* edited by P. Occhiogrosso, 79-87. Boston, MA: Houghton Mufflin.

Torry, Robert H. 1987. The McCurdy mission school story. *Methodist History* 25 (January): 111-126.

Trabold, Robert. 1989. Algunas reflexiones sociológicas sobre la religión festivo-popular caribeña de Nueva York. *Cristianismo y Sociedad* 27, no. 100 (3ra época): 55-70.

Traverzo, David. 1989. Towards a theology of mission in the U.S. Puerto Rican migrant community: From captivity to liberation. *Apuntes: Reflexiones Teológicas desde el Margen Hispano* 9 (Fall): 51-59.

_____. 1994a. La religión latina en Estados Unidos: Luchas pasadas y tendencias presentes. *Cristianismo y Sociedad* [Guayaquil, Ecuador] 31-32, no. 118-119: 79-94.

_____. 1994b. A paradigm for contemporary Latino thought and praxis: Orlando E. Costas's Latino radical evangelical approach. *Latino Studies Journal* 5, no. 3 (September): 108-131.

Turner, Kay F. 1982. Mexican-American home altars: Toward their interpretation. *Aztlan* 13, no. 1,2 (Spring/Fall): 304-326.

Urrabazo, Rosendo. 1992. Pastoral education of Hispanic adults. *Missiology* 20, no. 2 (April): 258-260.

_____. 1992. Pastoral ministry in a multicultural society. *Origins* 22, no. 23 (November 19): 386-391.

Vázquez, Edmundo E. 1989. Hispanic urban ministry comes of age. *The Christian Ministry* 20 (March-April): 20-21.

Vidal, Jaime R. 1982. "Popular religion in the lands of origin of New York's Hispanic population." In *Hispanics in New York: Religious, cultural, and social experiences,* Vol. 2, edited by Ruth Doyle and Olga Scarpetta, 1-48. New York: Office of Pastoral Research of the Archdiocese of New York.

_____. 1988. "Popular religion among the Hispanics in the general area of the Archdiocese of Newark." In *Presencia nueva: A study of Hispanics in the Archdiocese of Newark,* 235-352. Newark, NJ: Office of Research and Planning of the Archdiocese of Newark.

_____. 1990. The American church and the Puerto Rican people. *U.S. Catholic Historian* 9 (Spring): 119-136.

Vigil, James D. 1982. Human revitalization: The six tasks of Victory Outreach. *The Drew Gateway* 52, no. 3: 49-59.

Villafañe, Eldin. 1993. *The liberating spirit: Toward an Hispanic American Pentecostal social ethic.* Grand Rapids, MI: Eerdmans.

Villa Parra, Olga, et al. 1982. "New visions for Hispanics." In *Theology in the Americas,* edited by Sergio Torres and John Eagleson, 123-126. Maryknoll, NY: Orbis Books.

Villarreal, Luis. 1991. Counseling Hispanics [cross-cultural counseling for Hispanic American families]. *Urban Mission* 9 (November): 33-41.

Villota, Luis. 1978. To honor La Virgen. *Nuestro* 2, no. 12 (December): 28-29.

Viramontes-Gutierrez, Theresa. 1991. "A look at confirmation through 'Spanish' eyes." In *Confirming the faith of adolescents,* edited by A. Kubick, 96-106. New York: Paulist Press.

Wagner, John A. 1966. "The role of the Christian church." In *La Raza: Forgotten Americans,* edited by Julian Zamora, [Ch.2]. Notre Dame, IN: University of Notre Dame Press.

Ward, James García. 1990. Project 13: Hispanic vocations and formation [in US Catholic Church]. *Apuntes: Reflexiones Teológicas desde el Margen Hispano* 10 (Spring): 15-16.

Wroth, William. 1988. New Mexican santos and the preservation of religious traditions. *El Palacio: Magazine of the Museum of New Mexico* 94 (Summer-Fall): 4-17.

Zambrano, Ariel. 1983. In the depths of the well, looking at the stars. *Apuntes: Reflexiones Teológicas desde el Margen Hispano* 3, no. 4 (Winter): 89-93.

Zapata, Dominga M. [1976]. "Gospel to the Hispanic: Unrecognized ministry?" In *Women in ministry,* edited by A. Cunningham, et al., 123-133. Washington, D.C.: Publications Office of the USCC.

_____. 1990. Ministries among Hispanics in the United States: Developments and challenges. *New Theology Review* 3, no. 1 (November): 62-71.

Reports, Documents, Newspaper and Journalistic Accounts, Unpublished Papers, and Bibliographies III

Abalos, David T. 1982. "The relationship between Latino religious patterns and political participation." Society for the Scientific Study of Religion, Providence, RI, October 22.

_____. 1984. "Latinos in the United States, the sacred and the political." Joint Meeting of the American Academy of Religion and Catholic Theology Society, Mid-Atlantic Regional Meeting, Montclair State College, March 9.

_____. 1985. "Holism, spirituality, and healing in minority communities." Series on Critical Issues in Mental Health, Health and Social Services, Seton Hall University, May 7.

_____. 1986. "Dominicans in the United States and the politics of transformation." International Congress on the Dominican Republic, Rutgers University, April 12.

_____. 1988. "Continuities and discontinuities of the sacred since the conquest." National Conference, Latinos and Religion in the United States, May 5.

Albizu Campos, Pedro. 1980. "Columbus Day speech, Ponce, Puerto Rico, October 12, 1933." In *Prophets denied honor,* edited by Antonio M. Stevens-Arroyo, 59-63. Maryknoll, NY: Orbis Books.

Allsup, Dan. 1987. A Texas hello for John Paul II. *Vista* 3, no. 1 (September): 8-9.

Alurista. 1989. "El plan espiritual de Aztlán." In *Aztlán: Essays on the Chicano homeland,* edited by Rudolfo Anaya and Francisco Lomeli, 1-5. Albuquerque: University of New Mexico Press.

Bishops Committee for the Spanish Speaking. 1962. *National Council for the Spanish Speaking.* Progress Report.

_____. 1980. "Report (May 1973) of the Ad Hoc Committee for the Spanish Speaking, National Conference of Catholic Bishops (NCCB), on the conclusion of the First Hispano Pastoral Encounter, held June 1972 (excerpts)." In *Prophets denied honor,* edited by Antonio M. Stevens-Arroyo, 201-207. Maryknoll, NY: Orbis Books.

Bonilla, Plutarco. 1989. "Viaje de ida y vuelta: Evangelización y misión—apuntes sobre el pensamiento misionológico de Orlando E. Costas." Puerto Rico. Mimeographed.

Boyle, Gregory J. 1995. "Hope is the only antidote." *Los Angeles Times* (January 6).

Cadena, Gilbert R. 1983. "Chicanos and Catholicism: Two perspectives for change." National Association for Chicano Studies, Eastern Michigan University, April.

_____. 1984. "Chicanas and church hegemony: Toward a liberation theology." National Association for Chicano Studies, University of Texas, Austin, March.

_____. 1986a. "The impact of liberation theology on Chicano clergy." National Association for Chicano Studies, University of Texas, El Paso, April.

_____. 1986b. "A study of Mexican American priests in the United States." LOS PADRES National Convention, Mexican American Cultural Center, San Antonio, TX, October.

_____. 1987a. "Chicano clergy and empowerment: A quantitative analysis."

National Association for Chicano Studies, Salt Lake City, UT, April.

_____. 1987b. "The Church as a support system." Fifth Wisconsin Conference on the Hispanic Family, Milwaukee, WI, September.

_____. 1988a. "Chicano clergy and liberation theology: A descriptive analysis." (SCCR Working Paper no. 23). Stanford Center for Chicano Research, Stanford, CA.

_____. 1988b. "Catholicism and Chicano resistance." Society for the Scientific Study of Religion, Chicago, IL, March.

_____. 1988c. "Religion and politics in the Southwest." Pacific Sociological Association, Las Vegas, NV, April.

_____. 1988d. "Religious leaders in the Chicano community: Organic intellectuals." National Association for Chicano Studies, Boulder, CO, April.

————. 1989a. "Challenging the sacred cow: Chicanos, the Catholic church, and empowerment." National Association for Chicano Studies, Los Angeles, CA, March.

————. 1989b. "Latinos and recent developments in the church." Cushwa Center for the Study of American Catholicism, University of Notre Dame, IN, July.

————. 1989c. "A socio-religious history of Chicanos and the Catholic church." American Sociological Association, San Francisco, CA, August.

————. 1989d. "A broken covenant: Chicano-Catholic history, 1848-1960." Society for the Scientific Study of Religion, Salt Lake City, UT, October.

————. 1994. "Latina/o stratification and institutional discrimination in the Catholic church." Society for the Scientific Study of Religion, Albuquerque, NM, November 5.

Cadena, Gilbert R., and Lara Medina. 1990. "From social analysis to theological production: Chicanos, the Catholic church and U.S. liberation theology." International Sociological Association, Madrid, Spain, July.

Carpio, Patricia. 1972a. Church revolt in Colorado: Mexicano Catholics say, no! to Catholic authorities. La Luz 1, no. 1 (April): 46.

————. 1972b. Mariachi mass: A cultural experience. La Luz 1, no. 2 (May): 34.

Carrasco, David. 1979. "The religious dimensions of Chicano experience." Chicano Studies Colloquium, University of California at Santa Barbara, Spring.

————. 1982a. "The Mexican-U.S. border as sacred geography: Terror and fascination in Chicano experience." San Diego State University, April.

————. 1982b. "Aztec ritual, Chicano reality." Centro Cultural de la Raza, San Diego, CA, April.

Carreño, Richard D. 1980. Regional report, politics: Mass, militant priest. Nuestro 4, no. 3 (May): 14-15.

Casey, Rick. 1980. "Bishops back barrio power." In Prophets denied honor, edited by Antonio M. Stevens-Arroyo, 230-231. Maryknoll, NY: Orbis Books.

Castellanos, Isabel. 1987. "The languages of Afro-Cuban religion." Seminar on Afro-American Cultures, American Museum of Natural History, New York, November 18.

"Católicos por la Raza: Open letter to Cardinal McIntyre." (n.d.) *La Raza Magazine* 1, no. 1.

Chávez, Gilberto, and Silvano M. Tomasi. 1980. The bittersweet experience of a Mexican-American bishop—an interview with Bishop Gilberto Chávez (excerpt). In *Prophets denied honor,* edited by Antonio M. Stevens-Arroyo, 349-351. Maryknoll, NY: Orbis Books.

Chávez, César. 1968. The Mexican American and the church. *El Grito* 1, no. 4 (Summer): 9-12. Reprinted, 1980, in *Prophets denied honor,* edited by Antonio M. Stevens-Arroyo, 118-121. Maryknoll, NY: Orbis Books.

"Chicano bishops speak out." 1976. In *El Quetzal emplumece,* compiled by Carmela Montalvo and Leonardo Anguiano, 324-327. San Antonio, TX: Mexican American Cultural Center.

Chicano churchmen: Servitude or support. 1971. *La Raza* 1, no. 4 (January): 53.

Christians for Socialism. 1980. "Position paper, Christians for Socialism, Puerto Rico." Excerpted in *Prophets denied honor,* edited by Antonio M. Stevens-Arroyo, 295-300. Maryknoll, NY: Orbis Books.

"Church vs. Católicos." (n.d.) *La Raza Magazine* 1, no. 1: 20.

Coll y Toste, Cayetano. 1980. Celebrated Puerto Ricans. In *Prophets denied honor,* edited by Antonio M. Stevens-Arroyo, 52-54. Maryknoll, NY: Orbis Books.

Cook, Joy. 1972. Bishop Patrick Flores: The barrio bishop. *La Luz* 1, no. 4 (August): 18-21.

Cordasco, Francesco, et al. 1972. *Puerto Ricans on the United States mainland: A bibliography of reports, texts, critical studies and related materials.* Totoa, NJ: Rowman and Littlefield.

Cortés, Carlos E., ed. n.d. "A report on the Protestant Spanish Community of New York." Dept. of Research Planning and Research: Protestant Council of the City of New York.

Cortés, Ernesto, Jr. Changing the locus of political decision-making: San Antonio's COPS. *Christianity and Crisis: A Christian Journal of Opinion* 47 (February): 18-22.

Creative Catechetics Workshop. 1974. "Possibilities for catechetics and liturgy for the Mexican American community." Mexican American Cultural Center, San Antonio, TX, June 9.

Day, Mark. 1982a. Immigrants...and Mexican citizens. *National Catholic Reporter* Vol. 18 (February): 3.

_____. 1982b. Hispanics want more bishops, input in church. *National Catholic Reporter* Vol. 18 (March 12):1.

Day, Mark, and Ricardo Ramírez. 1982. Bishop: Why have we had to wait so long for Hispanic leaders. *National Catholic Reporter* Vol. 19 (December 24): 6-7.

De Diego, José. 1980. "For God and Country." In *Prophets denied honor,* edited by Antonio M. Stevens-Arroyo, 50-52. Maryknoll, NY: Orbis Books.

Del Castillo Guilbault, Rose. 1990. Women, church, choice. *This World* (Sunday supplement-San Francisco Chronicle/Examiner) (October 21): 2,4.

Díaz del Castillo, Bernal. 1963. *The conquest of New Spain,* translated by J.M. Cohen. New York: Penguin.

Díaz-Stevens, Ana María. 1984. "The Spanish speaking apostolate in New York: An historical context for the missionary concept in urban Catholicism." Spring meeting of the American Catholic Historical Association, Villanova University, April 14.

_____. 1987a. "The Puerto Rican migration from the beginning of this century to the present." The Museum of Natural History, NY, February 23.

_____. 1987b. "Pastoral practices and cultural identity: The role of the Post-Conciliar church. Society for the Scientific Study of Religion, Louisville, KY, October 31.

_____. 1988a. "The churches: A labyrinth for the Latin woman." Colloquium on the Dimensions of the Latino Religious Experience in the United States, Princeton University, May.

_____. 1988b. "Conflict in Comerío: Socio-political meaning of liturgical symbols." Society for the Scientific Study of Religion, Chicago, IL, October 30.

_____. 1989a. "La Misa Jíbara as an ideological battlefield." Prepared for the XV International Congress, Latin American Studies Association (LASA), San Juan, Puerto Rico, September 22.

_____. 1989b. "The pastoral influence of 'Hispano': Neutralizing nationalism in the Catholic archdiocese of New York." Society for the Scientific Study of Religion, Salt Lake City, UT, October 28.

_____. 1990a. "Social distance and religious conflict in the Pre-Vatican Catholicism of Puerto Rico." Middle Atlantic Council of Latin American Studies (MACLAS), Rutgers University, April 6.

_____. 1990b. "American Catholicism's encounter with the religion of the Puerto Rican people: A socio-historic interpretation." A working paper presented at the Cushwa Center for the Study of American Catholicism of Notre Dame University, September 27.

_____. 1990c. "After twenty years...The direction of Latino church leadership." Society for the Scientific Study of Religion, Virginia Beach, VA, November 10.

_____. 1991. "Analyzing folk customs for socio-political meaning." First conference meeting of Program for the Analysis of Religion Among Latinos (PARAL), University Village at Chicago, April 12.

_____. 1992a. "El impacto de la religión en la experiencia de los puertorriqueños en Nueva York." Special Invited Guest of El Centro de Investigaciones Sociales and El Departamento de Sociología y Antropología de la Facultad de Ciencias Sociales de la Universidad de Puerto Rico, January 28.

_____. 1992b. "The Latina woman as priestess and prophetess of popular religion." Thirteenth meeting of the Middle Atlantic Council of Latin American Studies (MACLAS), University of Maryland, College Park, April 4.

_____. 1992c. "Assessing the matriarchal core of Latino Popular religion." Association for the Sociology of Religion, Pittsburgh, PA, August 18.

Díaz-Stevens, Ana María, and Anthony M. Stevens-Arroyo. 1988. "Fiestas Patronales as a community process: The Puerto Rican experience." Religious Research Association (RRA), Chicago, IL, October 29.

_____. 1994. "Religious tradition and subversive politics: A Gramscian perspective on Puerto Rican popular religiosity." Society for the Scientific Study of Religion, Albuquerque, NM, November 4.

"Editorial: The Second Encounter." 1980. In *Prophets denied honor,* edited by Antonio M. Stevens-Arroyo, 325-326. Maryknoll, NY: Orbis Books.

"Encuentro." 1973. *La Luz* 2, no. 2 (May): 24

Executive Committee of Home Missions Synod of Texas Presbyterian Church, U.S. 1946. *Flying chips: Latin American Presbyterianism in Texas.* Home Missions Synod of Texas.

Far West region: UNO - a voice from East Los Angeles. 1978. *La Luz* 7, no. 10 (October): 32-33.

Fitzpatrick, Joseph P., and Douglas T. Gurak. 1979. *Hispanic intermarriage in New York City: 1975.* Monograph no. 2. Bronx, NY: Hispanic Research Center at Fordham University.

"Forge of unity [the]." 1980. In *Prophets denied honor,* edited by Antonio M. Stevens-Arroyo, 175-179. Maryknoll, NY: Orbis Books.

Fowley-Flores, Fay. 1990. *Annotated bibliography of Puerto Rican bibliographies.* Westport, CT: Greenwood Press.

Gann, Lewis, and Peter J. Duignan. 1987. Latinos and the Catholic Church in America. *Nuestro* 11, no. 4 (May): 10-13.

Garcia, Freddie, and Ninfa Garcia. 1988. "Born again." In *Outcry in the barrio.* San Antonio: Freddie Garcia Ministries.

Garcia, Rudy. 1977a. The Catholic church looks for a new Latino way. *Nuestro* 1, no. 7 (October).

_____. 1977b. How discrimination was made legal. *Nuestro* 1, no. 9 (December): 60-62.

Gastón, María Luisa. 1978a. Hispanic Catholics edition. *La Luz* 7, no. 10 (October).

_____. 1978b. Renaissance of Hispanic participation in the Catholic church. *La Luz* 7, no. 10 (October): 8-10.

"Genesis and statement of purpose of the planning committee for the First National Hispano Pastoral Encounter." 1980. In *Prophets denied honor,* edited by Antonio M. Stevens-Arroyo, 181-183. Maryknoll, NY: Orbis Books.

Golphin, Vincent F.A. 1985. At encuentro, vision, debate molds future. *National Catholic Reporter* 21, no. 38 (August 30): 1.

González, Rodolfo "Corky". 1967. "Yo soy Joaquín." El Gallo Newspaper. Excerpted, 1980, in *Prophets denied honor,* edited by Antonio M. Stevens Arroyo, 15-20. Maryknoll, NY: Orbis Books.

Hall, Suzanne, and Carleen Reck, eds. 1987. *Integral education: A response to the Hispanic presence.* Washington, D.C.: National Catholic Educational Association.

Hansen, Laurie. 1990. Hispanic population growing in dioceses. *Denver Catholic Register,* November 14.

Hartley, Loyde H. 1992. *Cities and Churches: An international bibliography.* 3 vols. ATLA Bibliography Series. Metuchen, NJ: Scarecrow Press

Hemrick, Eugene, ed. 1992. *Strangers and aliens no longer.* Part one: "The Hispanic presence in the Church of the United States." Washington, D.C.: NCCB/USCC Office of Research.

Hernández, Edwin. 1988. "Eschatological hope and the Hispanic evangelical experience." Society for the Scientific Study of Religion, Chicago, IL, October 30.

_____. 1991. "Hung between two worlds: The experience of second generation Hispanics." Annual John Osborne Lecturership, La Sierra University, La Sierra, CA, October 29.

_____. 1992. "An assessment of the problems, needs, and challenges of ministry to and with Hispanics." Hispanic Consultation in the Religion Division of the Lilly Endowment, January 9.

_____. 1994a. "Exploring the linkage of religion and social political issues among Latino conservative Christians: Evidence from a national study of Latino Adventists." Society for the Scientific Study of Religion, Albuquerque, NM, November 4.

_____. 1994b. "Latino youth, the Seventh Day Adventist Church and social justice issues: Interpretations of survey data." Society for the Scientific Study of Religion, Albuquerque, NM, November 6.

"Hispanic laity at work." 1978. La Luz 7, no. 10 (October): 29.

"Hispanic lay movements promote family values." 1978. La Luz 7, no. 10 (October): 45.

"Hispanic nun receives Rockefeller award for revitalizing Puerto Rican community." 1980. La Luz 8, no. 8 (October- November): 18-19.

"Hispanic youth organize nationally." 1978. La Luz 7, no. 10 (October): 41.

"Hispanics call U.S. church to action." 1988. The Witness 71 (November): 16-17.

"Hispanics keep the faith, but better parish work is needed." 1982. Migration Today 10, no. 5: 35.

"Hispanics meet to examine how U.S. churches respond to them." 1984. Christianity Today 28, no. 13 (September 21): 79-80.

"Hispanos and the church." 1978. La Luz 7, no. 10 (October/ September): 39.

"Hispanos and the church: Ten million Hispanics in the U.S." 1978. La Luz 7, no. 9 (September): 39.

Iglesias, María, and María Luz Hernández. 1980. "Hermanas". In Prophets denied honor, edited by Antonio M. Stevens-Arroyo, 141-142. Maryknoll, NY: Orbis Books.

Isais-A., Raoul E. 1979. "The Chicano and the American Catholic Church." Grito del Sol 4: 9-24.

Jadot, Jean. 1980. "Signs of the times." In *Prophets denied honor,* edited by Antonio M. Stevens-Arroyo, 344-347. Maryknoll, NY: Orbis Books.

Johnston, Robert L. 1988. Study urges Church to stress migrant empowerment, self-determination. *Migration World Magazine* 16, no. 3: 35.

Kosmin, Barry A., and Ariela Keysar. 1992. "Party political preferences of U.S. Hispanics: The varying impact of religion, social class and demographic factors." The Graduate School and University Center of the City University of New York, October.

"L.A. welcomes Hispanic home." 1986. *National Catholic Reporter* 22, no. 33 (June 20): 14.

"Lay people's encounter workshops." 1980. In *Prophets denied honor,* edited by Antonio M. Stevens-Arroyo, 146-150. Maryknoll, N.Y.: Orbis Books.

"Local priest leads Catholic opposition to FLOC." 1980. In *Prophets denied honor,* edited by Antonio M. Stevens-Arroyo, 328-329. Maryknoll, NY: Orbis Books.

"Los Mariachis sing the mass: Mexican folk music puts more into the mass." 1972. *La Luz* 1, no. 2 (May): 34-37.

"Los Padres: Hispano priests organize." 1973. *La Luz* 2, no. 2 (May): 6-10.

MacCorkle, Lyn. 1984. *Cubans in the United States: A bibliography for research in the social and behavioral sciences, 1960-1983.* Westport, CT: Greenwood Press.

"Mariachi mass: A cultural experience". 1972. *La Luz* 1, no. 2 (May): 63.

Marín, Gerardo, and Raymond J. Gamba. 1990. *Expectations and experiences of Hispanic Catholics and converts to Protestant churches.* San Francisco, CA: University of San Francisco, Social Psychology Laboratory, Technical Report no. 2, February.

Martínez, Douglas. 1979. Tomorrow: The growing campaign to conquer injustice. *Nuestro* 3, no. 6 (August): 62-63.

Martínez, Rubén. 1995. Virgin nation. *San Francisco Weekly* (January 4): 9-10.

McNamara, Patrick. 1993. "Researching churches in the Southwestern Latino community: How do the assumptions, theories and methods of twenty-five years ago stand today?" Society for the Scientific Study of Religion, Raleigh, NC, October.

Medina, Lara. 1987. "A Chicana experience of Tonantzín- Guadalupe."
    Pacific School of Religion, Graduate School of Theology, December.
    _____. 1989a. "Ceremonia de maíz y la vida." National Association
    for Chicano Studies, Los Angeles, CA, March.
    _____. 1989b. "A contribution to a Chicano\Chicana liberation
    theology." National Association for Chicano Studies, Los Angeles,
    CA, March.
    _____. 1989c. "Chicana spiritual theology." Sociologists for
    Women in Society, Berkeley, CA, August.
    _____. 1989d. "The Chicano community and the sacred." Society
    for the Scientific Study of Religion (SSSR), Salt Lake City, UT,
    October.
    _____. 1990a. "Chicana liberation spirituality." Mujeres Activas
    en Letras y Cambio Social (MALCS), University of California,
    Davis, March.
    _____. 1990b. "Integrating traditional religious beliefs with the
    contemporary struggle for liberation." National Association for
    Chicano Studies, Albuquerque, NM, March.
    _____. 1990c. "Chicano liberation spirituality and theology:
    Linking spirituality and politics in the Chicano community."
    Association for the Sociology of Religion, Washington, D.C., August.
    _____. 1991. "Chicanos, the Catholic church, and U.S. liberation
    theology. American Studies Connecting with Religion, University of
    California, Los Angeles, May.
    _____. 1992. "Chicana/Latina ritual." National Association for
    Chicano Studies Conference, San Antonio, TX, March.
    _____. 1994. "Latinas reclaiming soul: Deconstructing the
    sacrificial deaths of Aztec godesses and female mortals." Society
    for the Scientific Study of Religion. Albuquerque, NM, November 5.
Méndez, Verónica, and Allan Figueroa Deck. 1989. *An annotated
    bibliography on Hispanic spirituality.* Berkeley, CA: Jesuit School
    of Theology at Berkeley.
Miller, Wayne C. 1976. *A comprehensive bibliography for the study
    of American minorities.* 3 vols. New York: New York University
    Press.
    _____. 1977. *A handbook of American minorities.* New York: New
    York University Press.
Momeni, Jamshid A. 1984. *Demography of racial and ethnic minorities
    in the United States: An annotated bibliography with a review.*
    Westport, CT: Greenwood Press.

Moore, Donald T. 1969. "Puerto Rico para Cristo: A history of the progress of the evangelical missions on the island of Puerto Rico." Sondeos 43 Centro Intercultural de Documentación, Cuernavaca.

Morales, Cecilio J., Jr. 1982. Hispanics are moving toward the front pew. National Catholic Reporter Vol. 19 (December 31): 11.

_____. 1983. The Bishops' pastoral on Hispanic ministry. America 149 (June-July): 7-9.

_____. 1984. Hispanics and other "strangers": Implications of the new pastoral of the U.S. Catholic bishops. Migration Today 12, no. 1: 37-39.

Mosqueda, Lawrence J. 1977. "Religion as a form of social control: Chicanos and Catholicism." Western Political Science Association, Phoenix, April 1. Revised version, 1982, Symposium at U.C.L.A., Chicano Studies Research Center, May 14.

National Conference of Catholic Bishops. 1983. The Hispanic presence: Challenge and commitment. United States Catholic Conference, Washington, D.C., December 12.

_____. 1987. National pastoral plan for Hispanic ministry. [Bilingual ed.] Washington, D.C.: United States Catholic Conference, November.

"National Conference of Catholic Bishops Report: More Hispano bishops needed." 1973. La Luz 2, no. 6 (October): 28-29.

National Council of Catholic Bishops. 1980. "Resolution on the pastoral concern of the Church for people on the move (excerpts)." In Prophets denied honor, edited by Antonio M. Stevens-Arroyo, 347-348. Maryknoll, NY: Orbis Books.

NCCB/USCC Secretariat for Hispanic Affairs. 1990. National survey on Hispanic ministry. Washington, D.C.: National Catholic Conference of Bishops.

_____. 1991. Input from dioceses on the status of the implementation of the National Pastoral Plan for Hispanic Ministry. Washington, D.C.: National Catholic Conference of Bishops.

Newton, Frank, Esteban L. Olmedo, and Amado M. Padilla. 1980. Hispanic mental health research: A reference guide. University of California Press.

Nogales, Luis G. 1971. The Mexican American: A selected and annotated bibliography. Stanford, CA: Center for Latin American Studies -Stanford University.

Norman de Sánchez, Lucy, and Pablo E. Sánchez. 1979. Latinos in parochial schools: Divine neglect? *Nuestro* 3, no. 8 (September): 42, 44.

Ocampo, Tarcisio. 1967. *Puerto Rico: Partido Acción Cristiana, 1960-1962*. Sondeos 2. Cuernavaca: CIDOC.

Office of Pastoral Research, Archdiocese of New York. 1982. *Hispanics in New York: Religious, Cultural, and social experiences—A study of Hispanics in the Archdiocese of New York*. Office of Pastoral Research, Archbishop of New York, New York.

Pantoja, Segundo. 1994. "Los sicarios: Religious rituals of Colombian drug lord assassins." Society for the Scientific Study of Religion, Albuquerque, NM, November 6.

Paul VI, Pope. 1980. "Message from Pope Paul VI to the Second National Pastoral Encounter, held in Washington, D.C., August 18-21, 1977 (text)." In *Prophets denied honor*, edited by Antonio M. Stevens-Arroyo, 322-323. Maryknoll, NY: Orbis Books.

Pérez y González, María. 1994. "Latinas and the practice of social justice in the barrio: Considerations on the Mission Society study." Society for the Scientific Study of Religion, Albuquerque, NM, November 6.

Pérez y Mena, Andrés I. 1976. "A synthesis of Puerto Rican Spiritualism and modern psychology." Meeting of the American Psychological Association, Toronto, Canada.

_____. 1994a. "Ritual violence in a society of cheapened life: The role of Santería within the barrio." Society for the Scientific Study of Religion, Albuquerque, NM, November 6.

_____. 1994b. "From religious syncretism to transculturation: The basis of multiculturalism." Society for the Scientific Study of Religion, Albuquerque, NM, November 6.

Pino, Frank. 1974. *Mexican Americans: A research bibliography*. East Lansing, MI: Latin American Studies Center—Michigan State University.

"Planning the Second National Hispano Pastoral Encounter, 1977." 1980. In *Prophets denied honor*, edited by Antonio M. Stevens-Arroyo, 316-321. Maryknoll, NY: Orbis Books.

"Prelude to Hispanic church leadership in the '80s." 1979. *La Luz* 8, no. 3 (August-September): 9.

"Preserve the faith and culture." 1980. In *Prophets denied honor*, edited by Antonio M. Stevens-Arroyo, 239-241. Maryknoll, NY: Orbis Books.

Price, Jo-ann. 1980. "Bishops for the Hispano Church." In *Prophets denied honor,* edited by Antonio M. Stevens-Arroyo, 242-243. Maryknoll, NY: Orbis Books.

Princeton Religious Research Center. 1988. *The unchurched American...10 years later.* Princeton, NJ: Princeton Religious Research Center.

Provincia Eclesiástica de Puerto Rico, San Juan, Puerto Rico. 1989. "Los Señores Obispos de la Provincia Eclesiástica de Puerto Rico comunican a los fieles católicos sobre supuestos acontecimientos religiosos en Sabana Grande" *El Visitante Dominical,* October 14.

Quintanilla, Michael R. 1977. Regional report, religion: From Texas with love. *Nuestro* 1, no. 2 (May): 58.

Rodríguez, Manuel J., ed. 1986. *Directory of Hispanic priests in the United States of America.* New York: Hispanic Heritage.

Rodríguez, Richard. 1986. Evangélicos: Changes of heart, changes of habits, the crusade for the soul of the mission. *Image Magazine* (October 26).

Romero, Juan. 1976. *Reluctant dawn: Historia del Padre A.J. Martínez, cura de Taos.* San Antonio: Mexican American Cultural Center. Excerpted, 1980, in *Prophets denied honor,* edited by Antonio M. Stevens-Arroyo, 81-85. Maryknoll, NY: Orbis Books.

_____. 1980. "PADRES: Who they are and where they are going." In *Prophets denied honor,* edited by Antonio M. Stevens-Arroyo, 139-140. Maryknoll, NY: Orbis Books.

Rosado, Caleb. 1990. "The role of liberation theology on the social identity of Latinos." Society for the Scientific Study of Religion (SSSR), Virginia Beach, VA, November 11.

_____. 1992. "Towards a theory of religion and power in the Latino experience." Society for the Scientific Study of Religion (SSSR), Washington, D.C., November 8.

Rosado, Caleb, and Lourdes Morales-Gudmundsson. 1992. "Machismo, Marianismo and the Latino Adventist woman." Annual meeting of the Association for Sociology of Religion, Pittsburgh, PA, August 20.

Roybal, Rosa Marie, and Paul Sedillo. 1974. A profile of the Spanish speaking within the hierarchy of the Catholic church. *La Luz* 3, no. 2 (May).

Ruth, Doyle. 1994. "Northeastern Catholics and justice: Hispanics compared." Society for the Scientific Study of Religion. Albuquerque, NM, November 4.

Sánchez, Pablo E. 1977. The Catholic church, labor, and the undocumented worker. *Agenda* 7, no. 4 (July-August): 37-38.

Sánchez, Roberto, et al. 1980. "Somos Hispanos: A message of the Hispano bishops of the United States to the Hispano Catholics in this country, to all Catholics of the United States, and to all people of good will (August 1977)." In *Prophets denied honor,* edited by Antonio M. Stevens-Arroyo, 360-363. Maryknoll, NY: Orbis Books.

Sandoval, Mercedes C. 1977. "The history of a religious complex: Different ecological settings—Collaborative aspects of Santería and orthodox health care." Symposium on the Transcultural View: A prerequisite to inter-ethnic (inter-cultural) communication in medicine, Southern Anthropological Society, Miami, FL, March.

_____. 1978. "Santería in Miami." 21st Annual Meeting of the African Studies Association, Baltimore, MD, October 31.

Sandoval, Moisés. 1978. "Hispanic challenges to the Church." Washington, D.C.: Secretariat for Hispanic Affairs.

Schick, Frank L., and Renee Schick. 1991. *Statistical handbook on U.S. Hispanics.* Phoenix, AZ: Orix.

"Second Encounter [the]." 1980. In *Prophets denied honor,* edited by Antonio M. Stevens-Arroyo, 313-315. Maryknoll, NY: Orbis Books.

Secretariat for Hispanic Affairs. 1986. *Prophetic voices: The document of the process of the III Encuentro Nacional Hispano de Pastoral.* Washington, D.C., United States Catholic Conference.

Silva-Gotay, Samuel. 1994. "Protestantism and social justice in Puerto Rico: Two generational perspectives." Society for the Scientific Study of Religion, Albuquerque, NM, November 5.

Solivan, Samuel. 1994. "Orthopathos and social justice: Political implications of Pentecostalism for Puerto Ricans." Society for the Scientific Study of Religion, Albuquerque, NM, November 5.

Stevens-Arroyo, Anthony M. 1974. *The political philosophy of Don Pedro Albizu Campos: Theory and practice.* Occasional papers #13, Ibero-American Center, New York University.

_____. 1977. *Caribbean Latin America: Historical-cultural Reflections on migration.* Northeast Pastoral Center for Hispanics, New York.

_____. 1979. "Puerto Rico and peace." Lecture at Mary House, *The Catholic Worker,* New York City. April 27.

_____. 1982. "Puerto Rican migration to the United States and its implication upon Resolution 1514(XV)." Testimony offered to the

Special Committee, Department of Political Afairs, trusteeship and Decolonization, Organization of the United Nations, New York City, August 3.

_____. 1983. "La mitología Taína y los arquetipos jungianos: Una valoración." XI International Conference, Latin American Studies Association, Mexico City, September 30.

_____. 1985. "The trickster image in contemporary Puerto Rican urban culture." 84th Annual Meeting, the American Anthropological Association, Washington, D.C., December 6.

_____. 1986a. "Warfare among the Taínos: From the defeat of Caonabó to the victory of Enriquillo." First Annual International Conference on the Dominican Republic, Rutgers University, Newark, NJ, April 11.

_____. 1986b. "Old wine in new skins: The phenomenon of resanctification." Fifteenth Annual Meeting, ISCSC, Santa Fe College, NM, May 30.

_____. 1987. "Puerto Rican independence as a Catholic crusade: The nationalist Party and armed resistance." Society for the Scientific Study of Religion, Louisville, KY. October 30.

_____. 1988. "Marxism and popular religion." Panel discussion with Harvey Cox and Bertell Ollman, Church Center at the United Nations, sponsored by Christians Associated for Relations with Eastern Europe, November 18.

_____. 1989. "Nuestros Indios." Lecture on the Taíno Indians at Casa de la Herencia Cultural Puertorriqueña, Manhattan, March 4.

_____. 1990. "A Latino critique of the post-ethnic Catholic church." Society for the Scientific Study of Religion, Virginia Beach, March 15.

_____. 1991. "Incorporation into the World System and into the Otherworldly System: A comparative analysis of conquest and evangelization in the Canaries and Hispaniola, 1355-1522." Twentieth Annual Meeting, ISCSC, Santo Domingo, DR, June 1.

_____. 1992a. *Catholicism as civilization: Contemporary reflections on the political philosophy of Pedro Albizu Campos.* Caribbean Institute and Study Center for Latin America (CISCLA) Working Paper no. 50, Inter American university of Puerto Rico, San Germán.

_____. 1992b. "Juan Mateo Guaticabanú, September 21, 1496: The first Native American conversion and Spanish policy in

Española." Meeting of the American Catholic Historical Association, Notre Dame University, March 27.

_____. 1992c. "The medieval conversion model and the first American martyrs, 1496." Thirteenth Annual Meeting of the Middle Atlantic Council on Latin American Studies, College Park, April 4.

_____. 1992d. "El estudio de los Taínos en el Caribe: Aspectos metodológicos." Academia de Ciencias de Cuba, Habana, Cuba, May 18.

_____. 1992e. "La cosmonogía aruaca en el Caribe." Casa de las Américas, Habana, Cuba, May 19.

_____. 1992f. "Evangelization and Indigenous religions: The two sides of enculturation." Fifth Annual Colloquium of the Academy of Catholic Hispanic Theologians in the United States (ACHTUS), University of San Diego, June 28.

_____. 1992g. "Beyond survival: The Taínos in 1992." Forum *Cultural Survival in the Americas: Conquest and Resistance in the 500 years,* City College of New York, October 15.

_____. 1992h. "The invisible presence of Taíno religion today." American Museum of Natural History, New York City, November 17.

_____. 1992i. "Las Casas and the Taínos." Latino Center for Culture and Arts, Rutgers University, New Brunswick, NJ, November 23.

_____. 1993. "The Latino Agenda: Deamericanizing and recatholicizing American Catholicism." Society for the Scientific Study of Religion, Raleigh, NC, October 29.

_____. 1994a. "Jaime Balmes: Author of Irish republicanism and Puerto Rican independence: Catholicism as a revolutionary force." Twenty-third Annual Meeting of the International Society for the Comparative Study of Civilizations (ISCSC), University College, Dublin, Ireland, July 7.

_____. 1994b. "Religion as political ideology: The Puerto Rican experience." Society for the Scientific Study of Religion, Albuquerque, NM, November 4.

_____. 1994c. "Green lands, green politics: The echo of the Amerindian legacy in the Caribbean at the approach of the millenium." Museum of Natural History, New York, November 28.

Suro, Roberto. 1989. Switch by Hispanic Catholics changes face of U.S. religion. *New York Times* (May 14): 1, 14.

Tapia y Rivera, Alejandro. 1980. "La satanidad canto XV, 25- 26." In *Prophets denied honor,* edited by Antonio M. Stevens-Arroyo, 88-89. Maryknoll, NY: Orbis Books.

Teltsch, Kathleen. 1992. After 500 years, discovering Jewish ties that bind descendants of Sephardic 'conversos'. *New York Times* 142 (November 29): 12.

Torrens, James S. 1993. U.S. Latinos and religion: An interview with Otto Maduro. *America* 169, no. 4 (August 14): 16-19.

Torres, Lala, Edna Zallas, and Annette Ramos. 1980. "Presentation by Nabori, Youth workshop, First Northeast Regional Pastoral Encounter, November 30, 1974 [excerpt]." In *Prophets denied honor,* edited by Antonio M. Stevens- Arroyo, 341-343. Maryknoll, NY: Orbis Books.

U.S. Catholic Bishops' Conference. 1981. "Los Obispos hablan con la Virgen (Carta Pastoral de los Obispos Hispanos de los Estados Unidos)." Revista Maryknoll. Maryknoll, New York.

_____. 1987. "National pastoral plan for Hispanic ministry." *Origins* 17, no. 26 (December 10).

United Farm Workers. n.d. "The plan of Delano: Peregrinación, penitencia, revolución." *El Malcriado* no. 30.

United States Catholic Conference Hispanic Committee. 1980. "A program in preparation for Christmas (excerpt)." In *Prophets denied honor,* edited by Antonio M. Stevens-Arroyo, 236-238. Maryknoll, NY: Orbis Books.

"Unity in pluralism: A statement from the Second National Pastoral Encounter." 1980. In *Prophets denied honor,* edited by Antonio M. Stevens-Arroyo, 323-325. Maryknoll, NY: Orbis Books.

Vidal, Jaime R. 1981. "Santeria and the Church's response." Pastoral Life Conference of the Archdiocese of New York, St. Joseph Seminary, Dunwoodie, NY, November 11.

_____. 1983. "Multicultural Christian education: Reaching out to Hispanics in the Anglo parish." Christian Education Conference of the Episcopal Diocese of Newark, Fairleigh Dickinson University, Teaneck, NJ, June 24.

_____. 1988. "Hispanic popular religion and the American institutional church: Opportunities and conflicts." Workshop on study *Presencia Nueva* for Hispanic clery and lay leaders, Newark, NJ, September 24.

_____. 1989. "Some characteristics of Caribbean popular religion in the U.S.A." The Institute for Hispanic Spirituality, Jesuit School of Theology, Berkeley, CA, August 10.

_____. 1990. "The pre-history of present-day Puerto Rican Catholicism." Meeting of CEHILA-USA, Santa Fe, NM, September 21.

Vivo, Paquita. 1973. *The Puerto Ricans: An annotated bibliography.* Bowker.

Winkelman, Michael. 1995. Ethnomedicine: The ancient future of healing. *Vista* 10, no. 11 (July): 6-7.

Theses
and
Dissertations

IV

Alvarez-Plaud, Milca C. 1991. "Revitalizing a Hispanic congregation." D. Min., Drew University.

Alvirez, David. 1971. "The effects of formal church affiliation and religiosity in fertility patterns of Mexican-Americans in Austin, Texas." Ph.D. diss., University of Texas, Austin.

Arbaugh, William C. 1985. "The Lutheran Church and Hispanic people in the perspective of liberation theology." D. Min., Pacific Lutheran Theological Seminary.

Arriaga, José Jesús. 1991. "A missionary call to Hispanic youth: Their mestizo identity as Hispanics and Catholics." D. Min., The Catholic University of America.

Arrunategui, Herbert. 1985. "Evaluation of the development and implementation of Hispanic ministries programs in the Episcopal Church and the role of the National Hispanic Officer." D. Min., Drew University.

Ashmead, Roy W. 1990. "A critical investigation with a view to address tension between African-Americans and Caribbeans at the Brooklyn temple Seventh-Day Adventist church (New York)." D. Min., Drew University.

Ayala, Silvester. 1981. "Pastoral counseling the Mexican American evangelical within his\her cultural context." D. Min., San Francisco Theological Seminary.

Baselza, Edward. 1971. "Cultural Change and Protestantism in Puerto Rico." Ph.D. diss., New York University.

Belury, William R. 1984. "Creating an independent Episcopal congregation in the neighborhood of an existing Episcopal parish." Thesis, Brite Divinity School.

Bengtson, William C. 1992. "Preaching for spiritual nurturing in the Anglo-Hispanic parish setting." Thesis, Lutheran School of Theology at Chicago.

Bronson, Luise F. 1966. "Changes in personality needs and values following conversion to Protestantism in a traditionally Roman Catholic ethnic group." Ph.D. diss., University of Arizona.

Bryan, Jesse D. 1980. "Developing a pilot Baptist men's missionary unit in a Hispanic church." D. Min., New Orleans Baptist Theological Seminary.

Burgaleta, Claudio M. 1992. "Can syncretic Christianity save? A proposal for a Christian recovery of the syncretic elements in Latin American popular religiosity based on Rahner's concept of anonymous Christianity." Licentiate in Sacred Theology thesis, Jesuit School of Theology, Berkeley, California.

Busto, Rudy Val. 1991. "Like a mighty rushing wind: The religious impulse in the life and writing of Reies López Tijerina (Chicano Pentecostalism)." Ph.D. diss., University of California, Berkeley.

Cadena, Gilbert R. 1987. "Chicanos and the Catholic Church: Liberation theology as a form of empowerment." Ph.D. diss., University of California, Riverside.

Caloca-Rivas, Rigoberto. 1982. "Hermeneutics for a theology of integration: Components for an understanding of the role of the Hispanic church in the United States." Master's thesis, Graduate Theological Union, Berkeley.

Camacho-Vázquez, Eliu. 1989. "Safe teams: Development, implementation, and evaluation of a pilot for an evangelism strategy for Hispanics in Florida." Thesis, Golden Gate Baptist Theological Seminary.

Campbell, Frances M. 1986. "American Catholicism in northern New Mexico: A kaleidoscope of development, 1840-1885." Ph.D. diss., Graduate Theological Union, Berkeley.

Caraballo Ireland, Elba R. 1991. "The role of the Pentecostal Church as a service provider in the Puerto Rican community of Boston, Massachusetts: A case study." Ph.D. diss., Brandeis University, The F. Heller Graduate School of Advanced Studies in Social Welfare.

Caraballo, José A. 1983. "A certificate program for Hispanic clergy and lay leaders in an accredited theological seminary: A case study with projections." Ph.D. diss., Drew University.

Chakarsi, George. 1991. "Bridging the cultural gap between parents and children of Hispanic descent living in the United States." D. Min., Talbot School of Theology, Biola University.

Cintrón-Figueroa, Jorge Nehemias. 1969. "The use of the Bible in selected materials of the Hispanic-American curriculum." Ph.D. diss., Boston University Graduate School.

Cotto-Pérez, Irving. 1986. "The design and implementation of a strategy for a congregational mission in Hispanic churches in the Eastern Pennsylvania Conference of the United Methodist Church." D. Min., The Eastern Baptist Theological Seminary.

Cruz-Martínez, Jorge. 1990. "Design and implementation of a Freirian/ base ecclesial community model for education in a Latino, Black and Anglo urban congregation." D. Min., Drew University.

Danta, Rosalía L. 1989. "Conversion and denominational mobility: Study of Latin American Protestants in Queens, New York." Master's thesis, Queens College, CUNY.

Daugherty, Clifford E. 1985. "Reasons given by parents representing various ethnic and national-origin groups for enrolling children in Christian schools." E. D. D., University of San Francisco.

Dávalos, Karen. "Diversity and multiplicity: Emerging ethnicities and religious rituals among Mexican-Americans and Puerto Ricans in Chicago, 1920-1991." Ph.D. diss., Yale University.

Davis, Kenneth G. 1991. "The Mexican American alcoholic: Alcoholic Anonymous as a treatment modality for the Catholic male of Mexican descent." Thesis, Pacific School of Religion.

De León, Victor. 1979. "The silent Pentecostals: A biographical history of the Pentecostal movement among the Hispanics in the twentieth century." La Habra, CA.

Delgado, Hector. 1989. "A strategy for developing a more effective ministry to the Hispanic community in southern California." D. Min., Fuller Theological Seminary, Doctor of Ministry Program.

Díaz, Carmen M. 1988. "Cross-cultural counseling: Considerations for pastoral counseling with Hispanics." D. Min., Union Theological Seminary.

Díaz-Stevens, Ana María. 1983. "The Roman Catholic Archdiocese of New York and the Puerto Rican migration, 1950-1973: A sociological and historical analysis. Ph.D. diss., Fordham University.

Dietrich, Gleann Mark. 1985. "Membership growth in United Methodist inner city churches." D. Min., Lancaster Theological Seminary.

Dodrill, Mark Andrew. 1991. "Christian youth ministry in Hispanic Chicago and Barcelona: An inquiry into similarities, dissimilarities and cross-cultural themes." Ed. D., Trinity Evangelical Divinity School.

Ellis, Ivan Cheener. 1938. "The origin and development of Baptist churches and institutions in southern California." Master's thesis, University of Southern California.

Espinoza, Marco A. 1982. "Pastoral Care of Hispanic families in the United States: Socio-cultural, psychological, and religious considerations." Thesis, Andover Newton Theological School.

Esponda Dubin, Hector E. 1992. "Religión y etnicismo (La política en la fe)." Ph.D. diss., University of California, Santa Barbara.

Evangelista, Ramón Antonio. 1988. "A theology of liberation as a basis for ministry in the First Hispanic United Methodist Church of Buffalo." D. Min., Drew University.

Felter, Unice. 1941. "The social adaptation of the Mexican churches in the Chicago area." Master's thesis, University of Chicago.

Fernández, Eduardo C. 1992. "Towards a U. S. Hispanic theology." Licentiate of Theology thesis, Pontificia Universita Gregoriana, Roma.

Flanagan, Sean B. 1971. "The Catholic social principles and Chávez: A case study." Master's thesis, Loyola University, Los Angeles.

Flores, Richard R. 1989. " 'Los Pastores': Performance, poetics, and politics in folk drama." Ph.D. diss., University of Texas at Austin.

García Leduc, José M. 1990. "La iglesia y el clero católico de Puerto Rico (1800-1873): Su proyección social, económica y política." Ph.D. diss., Catholic University of America.

García, Osvaldo B. 1982. "Ministry to the Hispanic community of the Pomona Valley." D. Min., School of Theology at Claremont.

Giménez, Román V. 1985. "A manual for training lay leaders for youth ministry in the Hispanic churches." D. Min., Fuller Theological Seminary, School of Theology.

González Nieves, Roberto Octavio. 1984. "Ecological, ethnic and cultural factors of church practice in an urban Roman Catholic church." Ph.D. diss., Fordham University.

González, Rocio Revuelta. 1988. "The impact of family support system and strength of religious affiliation on levels of alienation and acculturation among Mexican-American adolescents." Ph.D. diss., California School of Professional Psychology, Los Angeles.

González y Pérez, Belén. 1991. "A reading of Orlando E. Costas on the theology of contextual evangelization: A Galilean perspective." Master's thesis, Lutheran Theological Seminary at Gettysburg, PA.

Guerrero, Andrés González. 1984. "The significance of *Nuestra Señora de Guadalupe* and *La Raza Cósmica* in the development of a Chicano theology of liberation." Ph.D. diss., University of California, Santa Barbara.

Harrison, David C. 1952. "A survey of the educational and administrative policies of the Baptist, Methodist, and Presbyterian churches among Mexican-American people in Texas." Master's thesis, University of Texas.

Hawkins, Wayne R. 1986. "Hispanic and Anglo Christians: A model for shared life." Thesis, San Francisco Theological Seminary.

Hernández, Edwin. 1987. "Selected variables related to religious commitment among church related Hispanic Seventh Day Adventist youth." Master's thesis, University of Notre Dame, Indiana.

Holland, Clifton L. [1974]. "The religious dimension in Hispanic Los Angeles: A Protestant case study." Ph.D. diss., William Carey Library, South Pasadena, CA.

Howard, Richard A. 1988. "*Proyecto pastoral:* A project in pastoral ministry with refugees and undocumented people." Thesis, Pacific School of Religion.

Hurt, Hubert Olyn. 1978. "The establishment of Hispanic congregations in the Bird Road and Riviera Baptist churches, Miami, FL." D. Min., New Orleans Baptist Theological Seminary.

Hurtado, Juan. 1975. "An attitudinal study of social distance between the Mexican-American and the church." Ph.D. diss., United States International University, San Diego.

Husband, Eliza. 1985. "Geography of a symbol: The Hispanic yard shrines of Tucson, AZ." Master's thesis, The University of Arizona.

Iregui, Camilo. 1991. "Individuation and the religious function of Latinos with HIV disease." Ph.D. diss., The Wright Institute.

Johnson, Perry L. 1992. "The dynamics of cross-cultural evangelism: An African-American-Hispanic experience." D. Min., Howard University School of Divinity.

Jordan, Brian J. 1990. "The formation of Hispanic Catholic lay leadership in the United States." Thesis, Andover Newton Theological School.

Kellogg, Josephine Anne. 1974. "The San Francisco mission band, 1948-1974." Master's thesis, Graduate Theological Union, Berkeley.

Knight, Robert Drew. 1989. "A study of the role of the Episcopal diocese of Los Angeles in meeting the psychosocial needs of Hispanics." M. S. W., California State University, Long Beach.

Lampe, Philip. 1973. "Comparative studies of the assimilations of Mexican Americans: Parochial schools vs. public schools." Ph.D. diss., Louisiana State University and Agriculture and Mechanical College.

Lockwood, George Frank. 1981. "Recent developments in U. S. Hispanic and Latin American Protestant church music." D. Min., School of Theology at Claremont.

Mangual-Rodríguez, Sandra. 1988. "The training of Hispanic Protestant preachers in the United States: An indigenous approach to homiletics." Thesis, Andover Newton Theological School.

Mark, Leslie David. 1982. "The role of seminary education in the development of spiritual leadership in the Hispanic American Protestant Church." D. Min., Fuller Theological Seminary, School of Theology.

Marrero, María Teresa. 1992. "Self-representation in Chicana and Latino/a theater and performance art." Ph.D. diss., University of California, Irvine.

Martin, Carlos G. 1992. "Evangelistic strategies of Seventh-Day Adventists to reach recent Hispanic immigrants to Texas: A critical evaluation." Ph.D. diss., Southwestern Baptist Theological Seminary.

Martínez, Juan Francisco. 1988. "Ministry among United States Hispanics by an ethno-religious minority: A Menonite Brethren case study." Th.M., Fuller Theological Seminary, School of World Mission.

Matovina, Timothy M. 1993. "San Antonio Tejanos, 1821-1860: A study of religion and ethnicity." Ph.D. diss., Catholic University.

McNamara, Patrick Hayes. 1968. "Bishops, priests and prophecy: A study in the sociology of religious protest." Ph.D. diss., University of California, Los Angeles.

Millán, Lara. 1989. "The Chicano community and the sacred: A contribution to a Chicano liberation theology." Master's thesis, Graduate Theological Union, Berkeley.

Miranda, Juan Carlos. 1982. "A church growth manual for the Hispanic community." D. Min., Fuller Theological Seminary, School of Theology.

Modad, Miled. 1989. "Developing and implementing a training program in public evangelism for lay members: Seventh-Day Adventist Churches Wisconsin Conference." Thesis, Andrews University.

Morrison, Suzanne Shumate. 1992. "Mexico's 'Day of the Dead' in San Francisco, California: A study of continuity and change in a popular religious festival." Ph.D. diss., Graduate Theological Union.

Mosqueda, Lawrence Joseph. 1979. "Chicanos, Catholicism and political ideology." Ph.D. diss., University of Washington.

Muñoz-Rivera, Brindice. 1989. "A pastoral counseling program for Mexican immigrant families." D. Min., School of Theology at Claremont.

Murrieta, Sara M. 1977. "The role of church-affiliated Hispanic organizations in meeting some significant needs of Hispanic Americans in the United States." Ph.D. diss., United States International University, San Diego.

Nasche, Teresa C. 1993. "Designing and implementing a program for training bilingual lay persons for ministry with Spanish-speaking patients in hospitals." Thesis, Brite Divinity School.

Neri, Michael. 1974. "Hispanic Catholicism in transitional California, 1848-1975." Ph.D. diss., Graduate Theological Union, Berkeley.

Ortegón, Samuel Maldonado. 1932. "The religious and social attitudes of the Mexican population of Los Angeles." Master's thesis, University of Southern California.

_____. 1950. "Religious thought and practice among Mexican Baptists of the United States, 1900-1947." Ph.D. diss., University of Southern California.

Ortiz, Carmen. 1988. "The influence of religious images on perceptions of femininity among women of Mexican origin." Ph.D. diss., California School of Professional Psychology at Berkeley.

Page, James T. 1992. "The development and implementation of a basic Spanish model for equipping Hispanic pastors to lead a marriage enrichment experience." Thesis, Golden Gate Baptist Theological Seminary.

Pankow, Fred John. 1986. "A scriptural stance toward undocumented Hispanics and selected methodologies for reaching them with the Gospel." Th.D., Concordia Seminary.

Peck, Rena Blanche. 1929. "The religious and social attitudes of the Mexican girls of the constituency of the All Nations Foundation in Los Angeles." Master's thesis, University of Southern California.

Peters, Tena Katie. 1980. "An investigation into the role of religious experience and commitment as a therapeutic factor in the treatment and rehabilitation of selected drug addicts from Teen Challenge: A follow-up study." Ph.D. diss., New York University.

Polischuk, Pablo. 1980. "Personality characteristics and role preferences among Hispanic Protestant ministers." Ph.D. diss., Fuller Theological Seminary.

Portillo, Carmen Julieta. 1990. "The process of bereavement for Mexican-American widows: A grounded theory approach." Ph.D. diss., University of Arizona.

Privett, Stephen A. 1985. "Robert E. Lucey: Evangelization and catechesis among Hispanic Catholics." Ph.D. diss., The Catholic University of America.

Pulido, Alberto López. 1989. "Race relations in the American Catholic Church: An historical and sociological analysis of Mexican American Catholics." Ph.D. diss., University of Notre Dame.

Remy, Martha Caroline M. 1970. "Protestant churches and Mexican Americans in south Texas." Ph.D. diss., University of Texas.

Rodriguez, Jeanette. 1990. "The impact of Our Lady of Guadalupe on the psychosocial and religious development of Mexican American women." Ph.D. diss., Graduate Theological Union, Berkeley.

Rojas, Dhalia Zuñiga. 1991. "Perceived health status, spiritual well-being, and selected health practices among Mexican- American women." Ph.D. diss., Texas Woman's University.

Rye, Gary C. 1977. "Hispanics and the Roman Catholic clergy: A case in conflict." Ph.D. diss., United States International University, San Diego.

Salomón, Esaul. 1991. "An experiment in visitation: A growing church in Hispanic ministry." Thesis, Concordia Theological Seminary.

Sánchez, Daniel R. 1991. "An interdisciplinary approach to theological contextualization with special reference to Hispanic Americans." Ph.D. diss., Oxford Center for Mission Studies.

Santoyo-Gamio, Raul. 1971. "The Mexican American and the Protestant ethic." Master's thesis, University of Notre Dame.

Savage, Peter. 1988. "Therapy in context: A descriptive and analytical overview of the Latin culture." Thesis, Andover Newton Theological School.

Sclafani, Juan M. 1989. "Seeking to improve the quality of marital communication for ten couples of *Iglesia Bautista* White Road." Thesis, Golden Gate Baptist Theological Seminary.

Selame, Claudio Alfredo. 1988. "The relationship between types and degrees of acculturation and worldminded attitudes." Ph.D. diss., California School of Professional Psychology, Los Angeles.

Shorack, John Scott Funk. 1990. "The life history of an undocumented Salvadoran." Master's thesis, Fuller Theological Seminary, School of World Mission.

Smith, Rosemary E. 1958. "The work of the Bishops' Committee for the Spanish speaking on behalf of the migrant worker." Master's thesis, The Catholic University of America.

Solivan, Samuel. 1993. "Orthopathos: Prolegomenon for a North American Hispanic theology." Ph.D. diss., Union Theological Seminary.

Solt, Marc C. 1993. "A manual of some factors involved in Hispanic urban church planting with reflections on personal experience." Thesis, Trinity Evangelical Divinity School.

Soto, Antonio. 1978. "The Chicano and the church in northern California, 1848-1978." Ph.D. diss., University of California, Berkeley.

Stark, Robert. 1978. "Religious ritual and class formation: The story of Pilsen St. Vitus parish and the 1977 *via crucis*." Ph.D. diss., University of Chicago.

Stevens-Arroyo, Antonio M. 1981. "The indigenous elements in the popular religion of Puerto Ricans." Ph.D. diss., Fordham University.

Sturni, Gary. 1988. "Models of theological education for Hispanic candidates for ordination in the Episcopal Church." Dissertation, San Francisco Theological Seminary.

Thies, Jeffrey Scott. 1991. "Mexican Catholicism in southern California: The importance of popular religiosity and sacramental practice in faith experience." D. Min., School of Theology at Claremont.

Tinoco, David Andrade. 1989. "Strategies for effective Hispanic ministries in Southern California by the United Methodist Church." D. Min., Fuller Theological Seminary, Doctor of Ministry Program.

Torres, Enrique M. 1981. "A challenge for the growth of Baptist churches in Los Angeles with emphasis on the Mexican American population." D. Miss., Fuller Theological Seminary, School of World Mission.

Torres, Walter Juan. 1980. "A comparison of Puerto Rican and Anglo concepts of appropriate mental health service utilization." Ph.D. diss., University of Colorado at Boulder.

Trabold, Robert Albert. 1988. "Neighborhood immigrant popular religion: A new interpretation." Ph.D. diss., City University of New York.

Traverzo, David. 1992. "The emergence of Latino radical evangelical social ethic in the work of Orlando E. Costas: An ethico-theological discourse from the underside of history." Ph.D. diss., Drew University.

Treviño, Roberto R. 1993. "La Fe: Catholicism and Mexican Americans in Houston, 1911-1972 (Texas)." Ph.D. diss., Stanford University.

Turner, Kay Frances. 1990. "Mexican-American women's home altars: The art of relationship." Ph.D. diss., University of Texas at Austin.

Urrabazo, Rosendo. 1986. "Interpretation and reflection on thematic apperception test and kinetic family drawing results of Mexican American teenagers." Ph.D. diss., Graduate Theological Union.

Vázquez, Raul A. 1991. "Contextualized theological education: Development and implementation of a basic pastoral skills training retreat for Texas Hispanics." Thesis, Golden Gate Baptist Theological Seminary.

Velásquez, Roger. 1982. "Theological education for Hispanic pastors in the American Baptist churches, U.S.A." D. Min., The Eastern Baptist Theological Seminary.

Villafañe, Eldin. 1989. "Toward an Hispanic American Pentecostal social ethic, with special reference to northeastern United States." Ph.D. diss., Boston University.

Walker, Randi Jones. 1983. "Protestantism in the Sangre de Cristo: Factors in the growth and decline of the Hispanic Protestant churches in northern New Mexico and southern Colorado, 1850-1920." Ph.D. diss., Claremont Graduate School.

Walsh, Albeus, C. S. C. 1952. "The work of the Catholic Bishops' Committee for the Spanish Speaking in the United States." Master's thesis, University of Texas.

Walton, Priscilla Ann H. 1981. "Community and the parochial school in the inner city." Ph.D. diss., Northwestern University.

White, Patricia Ruth. 1993. "Phenomenological case studies of four Hispanic and four non-Hispanic near-death experiences." Ph.D. diss., The Union Institute.

Willard, Francis Burleigh, Sr. 1984. "A proposal for the training of lay ministers for Hispanic Free Methodist Churches." D. Min., Fuller Theological Seminary, School of Theology.

Wright, Robert E. 1992. "Popular and official religiosity: A theoretical analysis and a case study of Laredo-Nuevo Laredo, 1755-1857." Ph.D. diss., The Graduate Theological Union.

Yohn, Susan Mitchell. 1987. "Religion, pluralism, and the limits of progressive reform: Presbyterian women home missionaries in New Mexico, 1870-1930." Ph.D. diss., New York University.

Youngman, Nilah M. 1993. "Affirming Hispanic women." Thesis, Austin Presbyterian Theological Seminary.

A Postscript to Librarians and Researchers

Kenneth G. Davis

Discovering Latino Religion, the final volume in the series published by the Program for the Analysis of Religion Among Latinos (PARAL) will make this area of research more user friendly. Scattered sources, often pursued on the basis of rumor or faulty memory, are compiled here in a single volume. Now if colleagues choose to pray, it will be from religious conviction, not scholarly frustration that 'please God' the library find a needed text on issues of Latino religion.

This postscript serves as the briefest of comments on how to profit from the bibliography and its related resources. I offer here a map through the classification of the very rich but complicated and sometimes even contradictory intersection between the variables of their religious expressions, and the somewhat chaotic mix of terminology used to describe them.

Take for instance, the name used to describe those persons living in the United States who trace their ancestry to Spanish-speaking nations of Latin America or the Caribbean. Terminology is not just an exercise in nomenclature but is also a value judgement. For instance, "Spanish" is a term that emphasizes a European trait at the expense of an indigenous one.[1] Any attempt at a pan-ethnic label sacrifices exactitude for convenience. After all, there are no actual persons who are Hispanic or Latino. There are only Puerto Ricans or immigrant Cubans or second generation Hondurans, for example. No umbrella term completely depicts each particularity.[2] Thus, the researcher must ferret through titles which use any of these nationality terms and understand that they are parts of a more general picture.

Even dealing with a specific subgroup is problematic. The population of Mexican descent, as the largest, serves as an example. First there are primary immigrants. Some remain only briefly, others are migratory workers, still others settle permanently. They differ due to the region of Mexico from which they come, the reasons for their coming North, as well as by racial, religious, and economic factors. Secondary immigrants, born in Mexico but raised in the United States, present another phenomenon as do second and succeeding generations. Immigrants may look down on Mexican Americans as *cholos* (or "sell-outs") while the native born may condemn immigrants as old fashioned and politically naive. Los Angelinos may consider Tejanos to be countrified cousins because of their rural roots. Hence even in a specific group there are great differences based on generation, social class, and geographical region. All of this affects both actual and ascribed religious beliefs and must be considered in the study of their religion.

But because each of these groups has more in common with each other than with ethnic groups in the United States which originated in Europe, "Latino" is a term one finds with increasing frequency in reference to United States residents: 1) whose ancestry includes both Spanish, and indigenous American and/or African societies and; 2) who have a historic connection to these cultures. A consensus seems to be forming among social scientists in favor of "Latino" as an appropriate appellation. Some have wondered if the term is too broad because in a technical sense, it includes at least Brazilians, Guyanese, etc. if not also Italians and the French.[3] And if Latinos are Latin Americans who live in the United States, then are we to exclude persons from the Caribbean? Are Haitians Latin Americans, and if not, are Puerto Ricans—citizens of the United States—to be considered Latin Americans? It is useful to consider the historical dimensions to Latino identity provided by the essay, "The Emergence of a Social Identity among Latino Catholics: An Appraisal," by Anthony M. Stevens-Arroyo.[4]

Whatever term we use then must be carefully defined. Latinos are not just Latin Americans living in the United States, but rather they include people of numerous nationalities, various generations, and great class, religious, and regional differences. This is why research into this area can be very complex, and even lead to a morass of conflicting or competing terms. One finds, for instance, that a slash with the grammatically correct feminine Spanish ending added so that we now have "Latino/a" as a term. Some standardized vocabulary would certainly help scholars from various fields, but the wait for standardization may be a long time in coming. Sensibly, the PARAL bibliography has included the many variations.

This is a wise choice because, while a standard term may be useful, researchers and bibliographers must also deal with particularities. Characteristics interact in different ways, making the study of Latinos a complex process of describing and categorizing variables such as: 1) level of acculturation and urbanization;[5] 2) generation and age; 3) socioeconomic class;[6] 4) gender; 5) geographic region; 6) particular ethnic ancestry; and 7) self-identification.[7] Likewise competent pastors and theologians must attend to considerations such as: 1) denomination;[8] 2) institutional and authority structures; 3) popular rites;[9] 4) *mestizaje;*[10] 5) sacramental moments; 6) charismatic movements;[11] and 7) the hermeneutic of suspicion.[12]

In the best of all possible worlds, of course, these different disciplines would work together in order to refine some common research paradigms by challenging each others prevailing assumptions. I call this "scholarly humanism." PARAL has served precisely to bring together these diverse disciplines in order to explore the religious expressions of Latinos from a rich mix of insights. The contribution of this bibliography lies in the fact that, gathered and arranged for the first time, are a wide range of previously scattered documents difficult to access, from various disciplines often not in dialogue with each other.

This is no small achievement. Research into the religious expressions of Latinos is an often tedious and always laborious process.[13] Any number of reference aids (e.g., *Choice: Current Reviews of Academic Books*) have no listing for Latinos. Specialized reference works (e.g., Gale Research's *Hispanic American Information Directory*) often commit mortal sins of omission in the area of religion. Online data bases are equally faulty. Internet, for example, has no listing for Hispanics or Latinos, nor anything under Mexican American. This means that one must hunt about under other headings (Mexicans in the United States? Latin American immigrants?) which, of course, diminishes its usefulness. Even the average bookstore, while shelving under titles such as "African American," or "Native American" rarely has a subject heading for Latinos who are shunted to "Latin America" or perhaps "General Ethnicity" (as if every book in the shop does not fall under that label!).

Moreover, scholars use a number of terms in confusing ways. For instance, some indexes list "Chicanos", others "Mexican Americans." Older sources note "folk religion", newer ones call the same phenomenon "popular religiosity." While these various scholarly dialects are rich in diversity, they make the work of bibliographers and researchers difficult. This is another reason for the need to classify this complicated and sometimes contradictory vocabulary through some accepted, interdisciplinary terminology.

Meanwhile, I have found that searching by authors is often a more expeditious approach, and in good databases truncating a term (e.g., "Cuba\") is helpful. Of course, when one can combine variables ("Puerto Ricans and religion") the field is much more manageable. Again, this is precisely why some standardized vocabulary concerning the variables presented above may be welcome; otherwise one can never narrow a search but must repeat it with a dizzying array of synonyms.

Hence, to retrieve, annotate, and categorize over a thousand titles on any subject concerning U.S. Latinos is a welcome scholarly event. To do so on a topic as important but also as ignored or misunderstood as religious experience, is a milestone. But this publication by PARAL is a beginning, not an end of the process. The PARAL series has opened the way to more competent and more systematized research in a literature that promises to grow rapidly. It would be wise to imitate the judicious categorizations suggested by PARAL rather than continue with the inadequate classifications that are all to frequent.

I would like to think that this bibliography and the other books in the PARAL series are an invitation to continue research on Latino religion. Each scholar becomes an artist. The bibliography supplies the various hues included in "Latino," and the range of colors found in their religious expressions, much as paint is arranged on an artist's palette. If we force ourselves to draw with tiny and careful brush strokes we may yet create a clear and detailed portrait worthy of the intricate yet still enigmatic face of Latino religion.

Endnotes

1. David Hayes-Bautista and Jorge Chapa, "Latino Terminology: Conceptual Bases for Standardized Terminology," *American Journal of Public Health* (77) 1988: 61-68.

2. At the same time it is important to note a common weltanschauung among all of these groups (c.f. Gerardo Marin and Barbara Van Oss Marin, *Research With Hispanic Populations* Applied Social Research Methods Series 23. Newbury Park, NJ: Sage Publications, 1991) as well as the fact that the United States of America may be witnessing the birth of some kind of pan-ethnic Latino or Hispanic. Are the children of Puerto Rican and Salvadoran parents, for instance, in some sense Latinos or Hispanics?

3. See volume 19, number 1 of *Latin American Perspectives,* as well as the special issue on Latino-Hispanic Ethnic Identity in the *Latino Studies Journal* volume 2 (September 1991).

4. In Jay P. Dolan and Alan Figueroa Deck, SJ, eds. in *Hispanic Catholic Culture in the U.S.: Issues and Concerns* University of Notre Dame Press: Notre Dame, 1994, pp. 77-130.

5. These terms include such variables as English and Spanish language proficiency, inter- ethnic marital status and preferences in friends, food etc and, in the case of religious experience, levels of secularity or adaptation to modernity.

6. This would include consideration, for instance, of levels of income and educational attainment.

7. Unlike ethnic ancestry, this refers to the subject by self-identifying with a choice of ethnic ancestry labels such as "Chicano" or "Mexican American". See Philip E. Lampe, "Mexican American or Chicano?" in M. Cotera and L. Huffurd, eds. *Bridging Two Cultures* (Austin: National Education Lab Publishers, 1980), 287-293.

8. See Julia Mitchell Corbett, "Religion in the United States: Notes Toward a New Classification," Religion and American Culture: A Journal of Interpretation 13 (1) Winter 1993: 103-111.

9. For an explanation of the intersection and competition between popular and institutional aspects of Latino religion see my article, "A Return to the Roots: Conversion and the Culture of the Mexican-Descent Catholic," in *Pastoral Psychology* 40 (3) January 1992: 139-158.

10. While this has become a key term in both Protestant and Catholic Latino theology, often its political, historic and indeed even ethnically specific connotations are not fully noted, nor is this applicable to all Latino groups. See María Pilar Aquino's "Directions and Foundations of Hispanic-Latino Theology: Toward a Mestiza Theology of Liberation," in *The Journal of Hispanic-Latino Theology* 1 (1)

November 1993: 5-21. In the same journal's second number (February 1994): 5-27 see Roberto S. Goizueta's "La Raga Cósmica: The Vision of José Vasconcelos." For a more pastoral rather than strictly theological approach consult the term as indexed in my book, *Primero Dios: Alcoholics Anonymous and the Hispanic Community* (London and Toronto: Associated University Presses, 1994).

11. This includes both the growing numbers of evangelical and Pentecostal Latinos, as well as similar movements within the Catholic Church. Allan Figueroa Deck, S.J. has often called for a greater appreciation of this aspect of religious experience as a needed nuance for liberation theology. See his article, "Hispanic Ministry: Reasons for our Hope," *America* 170 (14) 23 April 1994: 12-15. For a critique of feminist approaches to religion consult Ana María Díaz Stevens, "The Saving Grace: The Matriarchal Core of Latino Catholicism," *Latino Studies Journal* 4 (3) September 1993: 60-78.

12. This is an epistemological stance which refuses to accept as normative doctrines or sacred texts without first attending to the context in which they were created. For an overview of how Latinos assess Scripture, for instance, see Jean-Pierre Ruíz, "Beginning to Read the Bible in Spanish: An Initial Assessment," *Journal of Hispanic-Latino Theology* 1 (2) February 1994: 28-50.

13. The fruits of some of this labor is available every March in my annual article, "U.S. Hispanic Catholics: Trends and Recent Works," published in *Review for Religious.*